Guide to Buddhist Sites in the Indian Subcontinent

By Joy Bose and Siva Prasad Bose

Contents

Dedication

This book is dedicated to all those who have been involved in the preservation and conservation of the Buddhist places in India and neighboring countries.

Preface

The Indian subcontinent is the birthplace of Buddhism. Here is where the Buddha was born, where he lived and died. Here is where the first Buddhist councils were established, where the first monks practiced meditation, where the first stupas were built, where the great monasteries like Nalanda were established, where scholars from elsewhere in the Buddhist world came to learn Buddhism and so on. The earliest historical sites related to Buddhism were here too.

In this book we provide an overview of historical sites related to Buddhism in the Indian subcontinent: including India, Sri Lanka, Pakistan, Bangladesh, Bhutan and Nepal. Here too, we only mention some of the most important sites, for listing out all sites related to Buddhism is virtually impossible on account of their great number. We have also covered holy sites belonging to all the important sects of Buddhism, including Theravada and Mahayana and Vajrayana or Tibetan Buddhism.

From ancient caves adorned with Jataka murals, to majestic stupas built by emperors and secluded monasteries perched in the Himalayas, the diversity and depth of these sites is truly awe-inspiring. While we cover some of the most historically important and well-preserved locations, it would be impossible to include every site touched by the Dharma. What is presented here is a carefully curated collection, guided by historical significance, cultural richness, and practical accessibility.

For the purposes of this book, we exclude other important Asian Buddhist countries such as Myanmar, Thailand, Vietnam, Cambodia, China and Japan for now. These may be covered in a separate book later.

For the purpose of covering the sites, we group them based on proximity. The author has personally visited most of the sites mentioned in this book in India, Sri Lanka and Nepal.

The aim of this book is to provide the prospective traveler and pilgrim an overview of the sites so that they too can visit and see for themselves. We hope this book serves as both a travel companion and a meditative journey, guiding the reader through landscapes that have been witnesses to the Buddha's precious teachings.

Acknowledgements

In preparing this book, the authors would like to acknowledge and thank the kindness of countless people who made all the travels to different Buddhist places possible.

In particular, the author would like to thank Ishan for information about monasteries in Sikkim, where he had traveled a few years ago. We would like to thank Jayawan and other Sri Lankan friends from UK for kindly including us in their pilgrimage to Bodh Gaya, Rajgir and Nalanda. We would like to thank Tshering Lodey for showing us around in Paro and Thimpu in Bhutan as their personal guest. We would like to thank Sarat Chandra Vegunta and friends for showing us around Nagarjunakonda. We would also like to thank Sandeep and Ankit, for showing us around Bodh Gaya sites. Sandeep has a travel company based in Bodhgaya.

Note: Unless indicated, photos of the historical sites (that are not mentioned as taken from Wikimedia) were taken personally by the authors or their friends. Maps are made by google my maps.

Chapter 1: Introduction to the main sites related to Buddhism in India and neighboring countries

In this chapter we discuss some of the principal sites that are related to Buddhism in the Indian Subcontinent.

1.1 Four main Buddhist pilgrimage sites

The Buddha in the Mahaparinibbana sutta in the Pali Canon mentioned the main four places of Buddhist pilgrimage. An extract from the sutta reads as follows:

"There are four places, Ananda, that a pious person should visit and look upon with feelings of reverence. What are the four?

"'Here the Tathagata was born!' This, Ananda, is a place that a pious person should visit and look upon with feelings of reverence.

"'Here the Tathagata became fully enlightened in unsurpassed, supreme Enlightenment!' This, Ananda, is a place that a pious person should visit and look upon with feelings of reverence.

"'Here the Tathagata set rolling the unexcelled Wheel of the Dhamma!' This, Ananda, is a place that a pious person should visit and look upon with feelings of reverence.

"'Here the Tathagata passed away into the state of Nibbana in which no element of clinging remains!' This, Ananda, is a place that a pious person should visit and look upon with feelings of reverence.

"These, Ananda, are the four places that a pious person should visit and look upon with feelings of reverence. And truly there will come to these

places, Ananda, pious bhikkhus and bhikkhunis, laymen and laywomen, reflecting: 'Here the Tathagata was born! Here the Tathagata became fully enlightened in unsurpassed, supreme Enlightenment! Here the Tathagata set rolling the unexcelled Wheel of the Dhamma! Here the Tathagata passed away into the state of Nibbana in which no element of clinging remains!'

The above extract from the Mahaparinibbana sutta of the Pali canon mentions the four places:

- Place where Buddha was born: **Lumbini**, in Nepal
- Place where he was enlightened: **Bodhgaya**, in Bihar state in India
- Place where he gave the first sermon after enlightenment, thus setting the wheel of Dhamma in motion: **Sarnath**, near Varanasi in Uttar Pradesh state in India.
- Place where he passed away: **Kushinagar**, in Uttar Pradesh state in India

Of these, Bodh Gaya is considered the holiest place in Buddhism since it was the site of Buddha's enlightenment.

1.2 Other important historical sites, from the lifetime of the Buddha

Another four important sites from the lifetime of the Buddha include the following:

- **Sravasti**, in Uttar Pradesh state in India: Capital of the ancient Kosala kingdom. Site of Jetavana or Jeta's grove, where Buddha stayed and preached for many years
- **Rajgir**, in Bihar state in India: Capital of the mighty Magadha kingdom in ancient India, ruled during Buddha's lifetime by king Bimbisara, a great patron of the Buddha. Site of venu

vana or Venu forest, where Buddha stayed a few times. Site of vulture's peak (Gridhrakuta), where the heart sutra, lotus sutra and many other important Mahayana sutras were spoken by the Buddha. Also, it is the site of the first Buddhist council soon after the Buddha's death or Mahaparinirvana.

- **Vaishali**, in Bihar state in India: Site of the republic of the Lichchavis, who were supporters and followers of the Buddha during his lifetime. Also site of the second Buddhist council.
- **Sankissa**, in Uttar Pradesh state in India: where Buddha descended after preaching to the Gods in Tushita heaven.

1.3 Important Buddhist historical sites after the lifetime of the Buddha

The historical sites from later Buddhism include the following:

- **Nalanda**, in Bihar state in India: Site of the most famous Buddhist university
- **Amarawati** in Andhra Pradesh state in south India: Site of a majestic monastery and maha stupa
- **Nagarjunakonda** in Andhra Pradesh state in south India: Site of a Maha stupa and various other stupas and ruins, partially submerged after the dam was built at the site on the river Tungabhadra in the 1960s, but many of the historical remains were rescued by archeologists and installed on a new island close to the dam.
- **Ratnagiri**, **Lalitgiri** and **Udayagiri** monasteries in Odisha state in east India: Important Mahayana monasteries
- **Dhauli** near Bhubaneshvar in Odisha state in east India: site of the famous war where emperor Ashoka defeated the Kalinga state and was so affected by the number of people killed that he converted to Buddhism.
- Sanchi near Bhopal in Madhya Pradesh: site of the **Sanchi**

stupa, built by emperor Ashoka, which was the model for many later Buddhist stupas in India and abroad.

- **Ajanta caves** and **Ellora caves** near Aurangabad in Maharashtra state in west India: sites of a series of majestic caves including paintings from the Jatakas, carvings of Buddhas and from the Jatakas and rock cut monasteries.
- **Kanheri caves** in Mumbai in Maharashtra state in West India: Site of another series of caves with many beautiful carvings and stupas
- **Bojjhanakonda caves** near Vishakhapatnam, in Andhra Pradesh state of South India
- **Sannati,** a site of Ashoka's stupa and edicts in Karnataka in South India

Other Indian Buddhist sites include:

- Nagpur: site of Ambedkar's **Deekshabhumi**, where the famous Indian politician and architect of the constitution, Bhim Rao Ambedkar, accepted Buddhism in 1950s along with millions of followers.
- Mumbai: for **Global Vipassana Pagoda**
- Sites in India important for Tibetan or Vajrayana Buddhism: **Bylakuppe** in Karnataka for **Sera monastery, Dreipung** monastery, **Namdroling monastery, Mungdod** in Karnataka for **Ganden monastery**. Dehradun for **Sakya Monastery,** Rewalsar in Himachal Pradesh for **Tso Pema** lake, **Rumtek monastery** in Sikkim for the most important Karma Kagyu monastery, Leh or Ladakh for many important monasteries.

1.2 List of sites in Nepal

The list of important Buddhist sites in Nepal include the following:

- From time of the Buddha: **Lumbini**, where he was born
- The great stupas of the Kathmandu valley: **Boudhanath, Swayambhunath**
- **Patan** near Kathmandu
- **Namo Buddha** in the south east of Kathmandu valley, 40 km from Kathmandu

1.3 List of sites in Sri Lanka

The list of important Buddhist sites in Sri Lanka include the following:

- The most important site in Sri Lanka is the Bodhi tree, **Sri Maha Bodhiya**, located in the ancient capital city of **Anuradhapura** in Northern Sri Lanka. This was the place where a sapling from the original Bodhi tree in Bodh Gaya was planted by Mahinda, the son of emperor Ashoka. After the Bodhgaya Bodhi tree was destroyed in India in subsequent centuries, it was re-planted with a sapling from this tree.
- Kandy is the latest site of the temple of the sacred tooth relic of the Buddha, **Sri Dalada Maligawa** or temple of the tooth.
- Cultural triangle: **Sigiriya, Dambulla, Anuradhapura**. These are ancient capitals of Sri Lanka and sites of many important Buddhist temples built over the centuries.
- Adam's peak or **Sri Pada**: Pilgrimage site in Sri Lanka where the Buddha was supposed to have visited and an impression of his foot can be found.

1.4 List of sites in Bhutan

The list of sacred Buddhist pilgrimage sites in Bhutan include the following:

- **Paro**: Sacred site in Vajrayana or Tantrik or Tibetan Buddhism, site of the Tiger's nest monastery, founded by

Guru Padmasambhava, revered in Tibetan Buddhism as the second Buddha.

- **Thimpu**: Site of many important monasteries
- **Bhumthang**: Site of many important monasteries

1.5 List of places in Pakistan

The list of places in Pakistan include

- **Taxila**: Site of a famous ancient Buddhist university and monastery.
- **Swat valley**: Site of many Buddhist ruins
- **Peshawar**: site of a Kanishka stupa

1.6 List of places in Bangladesh

The list of Buddhist sites in Bangladesh include the following:

- **Somapura Mahavihara**: site of an ancient Buddhist monastery and university.
- **Jagaddala Mahavihara**: Site of another important ancient Buddhist monastery

1.7 Some good books to learn about Buddhist pilgrimage and important Buddhist sites

Some good books to learn about Buddhist pilgrimage and important Buddhist sites in more detail include the following:

- Best Foot Forward: A Pilgrim's Guide to the Sacred Sites of the Buddha by Dzongsar Jamyang Khyentse. Shambhala. Available from download from https://khyentsefoundation.org/preview-of-rinpoches-new-book-available-for-download/

- Holy Places of the Buddha, Crystal Mirror Series, Volume 9. By Tarthang Tulku and Elizabeth Cook. Dharma Pub.
- Along the Path: The Meditator's Companion to the Buddha's Land by Kory Goldberg and Michelle Décary. Pariyatti Press
- Buddhist India Rediscovered by Aruna Deshpande. Jaico Publishing House
- An excellent free online course on Buddhist Tourism offered by Swayam and coordinated by Central Institute Of Higher Tibetan Studies (CIHTS), Sarnath, Varanasi https://onlinecourses.swayam2.ac.in/ugc23_ge09/preview
- Buddhist Pilgrimage by Chan Khoon San. Buddhanet. Available for download at https://www.buddhanet.net/pdf_file/buddhistpilgrimage.pdf

1.8 Conclusion

In this chapter, we have discussed some important historical and other significant sites for Buddhism in the Indian subcontinent. In the coming chapters, we will discuss each of these sites in more detail.

Chapter 2: How to visit a Buddhist Pilgrimage Site

In this chapter we discuss some tips from Buddhist masters about how to behave when visiting a Buddhist pilgrimage place.

2.1 Being respectful

The first important practice is to be respectful at Buddhist holy sites. We should not treat it as some sort of picnic but as a place to meditate and contemplate on impermanence, suffering and other important Buddhist teachings. One should dress respectfully, treat the artifacts respectfully, walk respectfully, be kind to everyone around.

2.2 Meditation

One thing we can do is to sit quietly at each site, feel the peaceful energy of the place and meditate for a few minutes. The meditation can be mindfulness meditation or vipassana meditation or whichever meditation one chooses. One can also do walking meditation at the holy sites.

One can also visualize the Buddha's presence at each of the sites and get the feeling one is chanting along with the Buddha and his disciples.

2.3 Chanting of sutras, suttas and mantras

One can chant various pali suttas, Mahayana sutras and various mantras either silently or softly, individually or in a group. The selection of which sutra or sutta is appropriate depends on one's meditation tradition that they follow. One can also chant the sutras that are relevant to that particular site which is being visited.

For example, when visiting to vulture's peak in Rajgir one may like to chant the heart sutra (sutra on emptiness, which was spoken in Rajgir), when visiting Kushinagar one may chant the mahaparinibbana sutta (Buddha's last sermon before he passed into nirvana), and in Sarnath one may chant the dhammachakkapabattana sutta (sutta of turning wheel of the dhamma).

2.4 Devotional practices such as offering flowers

Offering flowers, incense, Tibetan white scarves or khatas, fruits and other devotional items at the specified places in the Buddhist holy sites is a good practice. Often, one can see plenty of flower sellers around the sites.

2.5 Offering money for upkeep of the sites

Another good practice is to leave a donation when visiting each of the sites, so that they can be maintained well. There are usually specified donation boxes for the purpose. Or else, one can donate to specific organizations like the Mahabodhi Society which are engaged in the upkeep of the sites. One can also donate to the monasteries which are often located close by, as a way of supporting the monks who are staying there.

One should also be kind to any local people at the sites, including the shopkeepers and people selling small items, people running the hotels, even the beggars.

2.6 Taking a monk or experienced practitioners as a spiritual guide

One option for groups is to take along a monk or experienced devotee or meditator who would be able to chant the correct suttas or sutras and practices appropriate for each place.

2.7 While circumambulating stupas

While circumambulating stupas it is advisable to do it clockwise. Have the feeling that you are circumambulating something which is very holy and precious.

2.8 Conclusion

In this chapter we have discussed a few of the activities one can do when visiting Buddhist pilgrimage sites.

Chapter 3: Bodhgaya, site of Buddha's enlightenment

In this chapter we discuss Bodhgaya, which is the holiest of the Buddhist holy sites, as the place where Buddha attained Nirvana or nibbana and became enlightened.

Figure: Location of Bodh gaya in Bihar state in north India. Latitude: 24.6951° N, Longitude: 84.9912° E

Location & Access

Latitude: 24.6951° N, Longitude: 84.9912° E

Nearest Airport: Gaya (approx. 15 km), with flights from Delhi, Kolkata and other cities.

By train: Gaya Junction is well connected. Dedicated Buddhist pilgrimage trains are available.

Best time to visit: October to February (cooler months).

Figure: Exterior of Gaya airport

3.1 Location of Bodhgaya and how to get there

Mahabodhi temple is located in Bodhgaya, which is in the Bihar state in North India. The closest airport to Bodhgaya is Gaya airport, about 15 km away, and which is served by flights from Delhi and Kolkata and other cities. One can also take the train from Delhi and elsewhere, or other means such as bus or private taxi. There are some dedicated trains for Buddhist pilgrims that are run by Indian railways, but it is sometimes difficult to find tickets on these trains, so it is better to book them as quickly as possible.

From Gaya airport one may take taxis to reach Bodhgaya, or take a shared auto.

Many hotels are located in Bodhgaya, of varying quality and price. One may stay in one of these hotels, but please be sure to check the actual distance of your hotel from Mahabodhi temple Bodhgaya on google maps. Alternatively, many foreign pilgrims choose to stay in one of the temple guesthouses that are located near the Mahabodhi temple.

Figure: View of the Mahabodhi temple complex

Figure: The main Buddha statue inside Mahabodhi temple

3.2 Mahabodhi temple complex in Bodhgaya

Mahabodhi temple complex is a UNESCO world heritage site and includes the main Mahabodhi temple, the bodhi tree and vajrasana or the seat where the Buddha attained enlightenment under the tree. The walls around the complex have scenes 1from Buddhas lives and the Jatakas and various dhamma quotes.

The complex commemorates the seven locations where the Buddha spent the weeks immediately following his enlightenment:

- Vajrasana — The Diamond Throne, site of the enlightenment itself.
- Animesh Lochana Chaitya — Where the Buddha stood and gazed at the Bodhi tree.
- Ratnaghara (House of Jewels) — Where the Buddha spent the fourth week in deep contemplation.
- Chakramana — The walking meditation path, marked by seven lotus stones.
- Mucalinda Lake — Where the great naga Mucalinda sheltered the meditating Buddha during a rainstorm.
- Rajayatana — The forest tree where the Buddha spent the seventh week.

There is also a meditation park inside the complex where visitors may sit in contemplation for a modest fee.

There is a security check before entering the Mahabodhi temple complex. Mobile phones, bags and shoes must be deposited outside. Cameras are allowed inside for a fee. In case you want a photo of yourself in front of the temple but do not have any camera with you, professional photographers are available who will take your photo from the steps in front of Mahabodhi temple and deliver the paper copy of the photo within 15 minutes for the fee of a few hundred rupees.

The main activities at the Mahabodhi temple complex is:

- Offer flowers, fruits and other offerings to the main Buddha state inside the Mahabodhi temple

- Peacefully meditate close to the Bodhi tree just outside the temple, the site where the Buddha himself meditated
- Silently or in a group do chanting of Buddhist sutras
- Circumambulation of the whole complex, in a clockwise direction. Or else, one can circumambulate just the Mahabodhi temple instead of the whole complex.

Figure: Ratnaghara or place of basic contemplation, in Mahabodhi temple complex in Bodhgaya

Figure: Mucchalinda lake, in Mahabodhi temple complex in Bodhgaya

Figure: Ashoka pillar in Bodh gaya

Figure: The author and friends in front of the Mahabodhi temple

Figure: Bodhi tree and vajrasana

Figure: Stupas in Mahabodhi temple complex

The Mahabodhi temple complex contains the sites of the miracles of the Buddha the first few weeks after enlightenment, including the following:

- The **muchalinda lake** where a large snake gave shelter to the meditating Buddha when it was raining
- **Rajayatana** or the forest tree where he spent the seventh week
- **Chakramana** or site of the seven steps of walking meditation circumambulations by the Buddha, marked by seven lotuses
- **Ratnaghara** or the house of jewels, where Buddha spent time in contemplation in the fourth week after enlightenment
- **Animesh Lochan Chiatya**: Where the Buddha opened his eyes

There is a meditation park inside the complex where for a small fee, visitors can sit and meditate.

Figure: Mahakala cave on Dungeshvari hill

3.3 Dungeshwari hill in Bodh Gaya

Dungeshwari hill or Mahakala cave is the place where prince Siddhartha, before becoming the Buddha, practiced severe austerities for 6 years before realizing the middle path.

There is a small Tibetan shrine dedicated to the Buddha in that cave, also a small shrine to the goddess Dungeshwari.

To climb the hill and reach the cave, one has to make a long walk of at least 30 minutes from the car park up the hill. The road from Bodh Gaya is quite bad even by car. Alternatively, there is a roundabout longer road to reach the hill from the outskirts of Gaya.

Figure: Sujata temple

3.4 Sujata temple

Sujata temple is in a small village on the outskirts of Bodh gaya, between Sujata stupa and Dungeshwari hill It's the exact tree under which pregnant Sujata and her maid gave milk rice or kheer to buddha who was going through austerities, thus saving his life. Burmese devotees have donated to build a small shrine here.

Figure: Sujata stupa

3.5 Sujata stupa monastery

This stupa was built during the Gupta period, but was unearthed (from an earthen mound) by the Archaeological Survey of India only in 2005 or later. Even after so many centuries it is almost intact without much damage. A tree is growing on top of the stupa.

If we are coming from the direction of Mahabodhi Temple, then it is situated across the river Niranjana or Falgu just after crossing the bridge.

It is a brick stupa in honor of Sujata, who fed milk and rice to the Buddha immediately after he finished his penance fast

Figure: Entrance to archeological museum in Bodhgaya

3.6 Archeological museum in Bodhgaya

The entry fee to the museum for Indians and foreigners is only Rs 10 in 2015 (subject to change). No photos are allowed inside the museum.

The museum has a small collection of the history of Bodhgaya from ancient times called Uruvela. During the time when the Mahabodhi Temple was being renovated, the railings of the Mahabodhi Temple from the Gupta and Shunga periods were dismantled and taken to this museum, where they are on display.

The museum also houses several Buddha and Bodhisattva statues in various postures: Dhyani Mudra, Bhoomi Sparsha Mudra. One can see that the art of painting has improved further over the centuries.

There is also a museum exhibit on how the Archaeological Survey of India restored the Mahabodhi Temple and how the Burmese kings also funded the restoration over the centuries. There were also sections on some Hindu deities such as the Sun God and Kubera, as well as on the Buddhist Tara and Jambala.

Figure: Mahabodhi society temple in Bodhgaya

3.7 Mahabodhi society temple

This temple is right next to the main Mahabodhi temple. It was built by Anagarika Dharmapala, the man who fought all his life for the restoration of the Bodh Gaya temple in the early 1900s. Pictures related to the life of Buddha are decorated on its walls. A plaque reads the history of the Mahabodhi Society and their struggle to save and restore the Bodh Gaya temple. The Pali Sutta is chanted by the monks every evening. The temple also runs a small medical center for those in need.

Figure: Giant Buddha statue in Bodh Gaya.

3.8 Giant Buddha statue

The giant Buddha statue is already about 40 years old in Japanese style. It is of sitting Buddha in meditation posture. It is located just next to the Japanese temple.

Figure: Interior of the Thai temple in Bodhgaya

Figure: Shrine room of Indosan Nipponji Japanese temple in Bodhgaya

Figure: Mongolian temple in Bodhgaya

3.9 Other temples in Bodhgaya

Since Bodhgaya is the holiest place of Buddhism, followers of every Buddhist country and almost every Buddhist tradition have built temples here. Interesting temples include Thai temple, Indosan Nipponji Japanese temple, Bhutanese temple, Root institute, Mongolian temple, etc.

3.10 Conclusion

In this chapter, we have discussed Bodhgaya, the Mahabodhi temple and other temples found around the Mahabodhi temple.

Chapter 4: Lumbini, site of Buddha's birth

Lumbini is the place where the Buddha was born. It is located in Nepal. It is a UNESCO world heritage site. It is built on a huge complex with multiple temples including Chinese, Sri Lankan, Burmese temple etc.

Figure: Location of Lumbini in Nepal. Latitude: 27.4844° N, Longitude: 83.2766° E

Location & Access

Latitude: 27.4844° N, Longitude: 83.2766° E

Nearest Airport: Bhairahawa (Gautam Buddha) Airport, approx. 25 km.

By bus or taxi from Gorakhpur (India), approx. 3 hours; or from Kathmandu, approx. 6 hours.

Best time to visit: October to March.

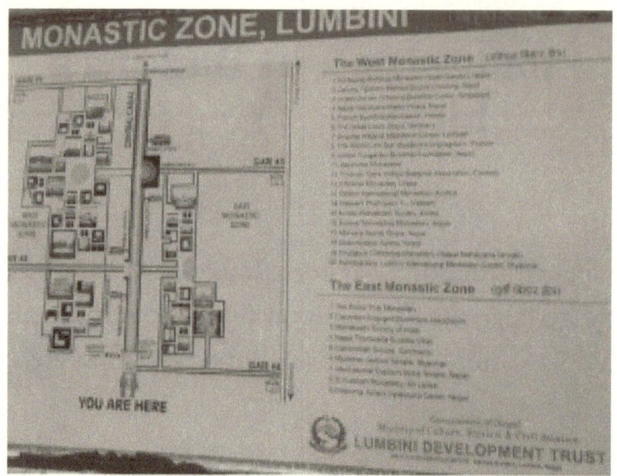

Figure: Poster showing a map of the monastic zone in Lumbini

4.1 How to get there

Lumbini can be reached on the bus from Gorakhpur or Kathmandu or alternatively by air. Lumbini airport is the closest airport.

Figure: Exterior of Mayadevi temple with ruins of a few ancient monasteries

Figure: Mayadevi temple from the outside

Figure: Ashoka pillar in Lumbini, outside Mayadevi temple

Figure: Pond in Lumbini next to Mayadevi temple

4.2 Mayadevi Temple

Mayadevi Temple is a World Heritage Site. It marks the place where the Buddha was born. Entry cost for SAARC foreigners is approximately 150 NR in 2019 (subject to change). We have to take off our shoes before entering and the floor surface can get hot in summer.

Taking photographs is not allowed inside the main temple, however photographs can be taken outside. It has a marker stone with the birthplace of Buddha, which is shaped like a womb. It has an Ashoka Pillar just outside the temple, there is also a Bodhi tree.

There is also a holy lake here. There are also many ruins of stupas dating from the 2nd century to the 5th century AD right next to the temple.

Figure: Thai monastery in Lumbini

Figure: Paintings from Buddha's life on the walls of the Cambodian monastery in Lumbini

Figure: Singapore monastery in Lumbini

Figure: Korean monastery in Lumbini

Figure: Nepali monastery in Lumbini

Figure: Chinese monastery in Lumbini

4.3 Other monasteries in Lumbini

There are many beautiful monasteries built by devotees from different countries in the monastic zone. There is a canal in the middle, and rows of monasteries on either sides of the canal. One can take a leisurely walk and explore each of the monasteries one by one.

4.4 Conclusion

In this chapter, we have discussed temples in Lumbini, which is the birthplace of the Buddha.

Chapter 5: Kushinagar, site of Buddha's passing away

In this chapter, we discuss Kushinagar, one of the four primary pilgrimage sites in Buddhism and the site of passing away of the Buddha. It is the location of Parinirvana stupa, the stupa built at the site of his parinibbana.

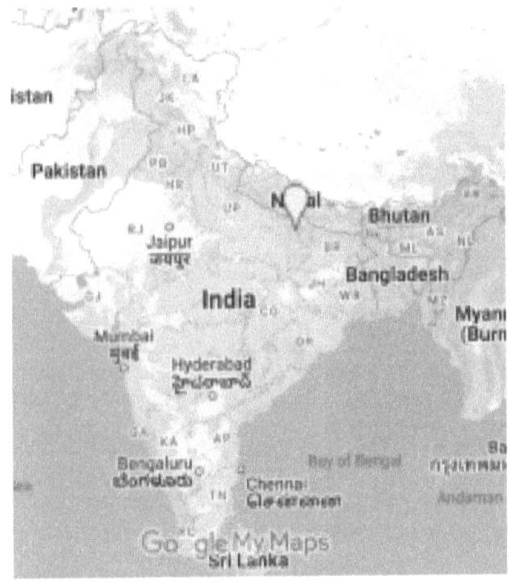

Figure: Location of Kushnagar in Uttar Pradesh state in north India. Latitude: 26.7397° N, Longitude: 83.8869° E

Location & Access

Latitude: 26.7397° N, Longitude: 83.8869° E

Nearest Airport: Kushinagar International Airport (approx. 8 km) — limited flights.

Gorakhpur Airport (approx. 50 km) has more frequent connections.

By train to Gorakhpur, then taxi or bus to Kushinagar.

5.1 How to get there

Kushinagar is located near Gorakhpur in Uttar Pradesh state in North India. It is close to India's border with Nepal. There is a newly launched Kushinagar airport which has a very few flights but is less than 10 km from the site, but otherwise Gorakhpur is the closest airport, and is about 50 km from the site. One can either fly to Gorakhpur or Kushinagar or take a train to Gorakhpur, which is well connected by rail to other Indian cities. From Gorakhpur, one can go to Kushinagar by bus or taxi.

Figure: Parinibbana stupa from outside

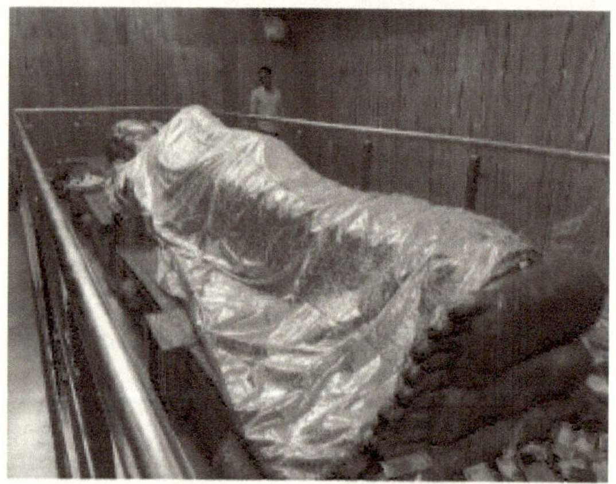

Figure: Statue of lying Buddha at Mahaparinirvana stupa in Kushinagar

5.2 Parinirvana stupa

The Parinirvana Stupa at Kushinagar is surrounded by several ancient monasteries. It is a very important site, which is celebrated to commemorate the Mahaparinirvana or Parinirvana of the Buddha.

It has a beautiful idol of sleeping Buddha inside the stupa. This was the posture of the Buddha lying on one side and meditating just before he died.

The grounds around the main stupa are covered with ancient ruins of votive stupas and monasteries. It is very hot in summer and feet tend to burn so it is better to wear socks, although we did have to deposit shoes before entering the main stupa complex.

Nearby is a museum and interpretation center where they have videos and posters explaining the history of the stupa and the life of the Buddha.

Figure: Exterior of Ramabhar stupa in Kushinagar

5.3 Ramabhar Stupa

Ramabhar Stupa, also known as Mukutbandhan Stupa, marks the cremation site of the Buddha. The relics of the Buddha were later divided among various kingdoms, leading to the construction of stupas across India.

This stupa is situated near a pond called Ramabhar and commemorates the exact spot where the Buddha was cremated, and his last rites were performed before the relics were divided between different kingdoms. It is a very old stupa but still in decent shape. There are lots of ruins of small monasteries surrounding the main stupa. It is not allowed to climb the stupa, but one can do circumambulation and light lamps in front.

Figure: Buddhist museum in Kushinagar

5.4 Buddhist museum in Kushinagar

It's a good Buddhist museum. Entry is just Rupees 3 for Indians in 2019 (subject to change). It also has a library, mostly closed, called Rahul Sankrityayan library.

One section has paintings on different events in Buddha's life. One has terracotta from Kushana and Gupta periods. One section has robes and daily utensils of a Japanese Soto zen monk, and some tibetan thangkas. Another section has Buddha statues from the Mathura and the Gandhara schools.

Outside of the museum building is a beautiful Japanese rock garden.

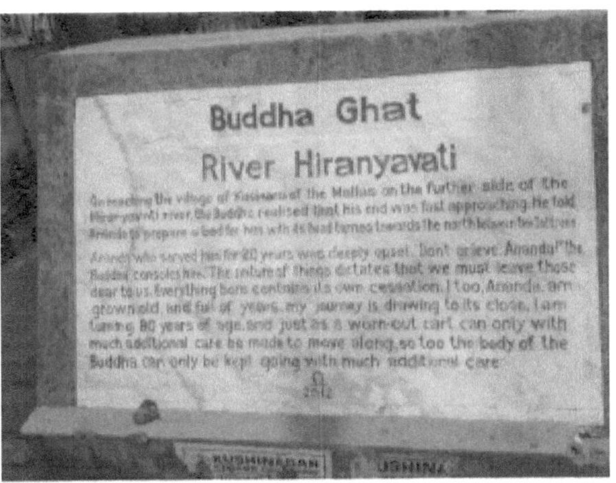

Figure: Sign outside Buddha ghat on banks of river Hiranyavati

5.5 Buddha Ghat

This is the place where the Buddha spent his last few days in the care of Ananda and other disciples after feeling ill. When Buddha was about to die, he fell ill near this ghat, near two Sal trees.

It is a well-maintained Ghat on the banks of the Hiranyavati River, next to the Rambhar Stupa, where he was cremated.

Figure: Exterior of Matha Kaur Shrine in Kushinagar

5.6 Matha Kaur Shrine

This was one of the earliest discovered shrines in this area, discovered in 1876 by a British officer and is the site of an ancient monastery. It is walking distance from the Parinibbana stupa.

Figure: Burmese stupa in Kushinagar

Figure: Interior of Thai temple in Kushinagar

Figure: Vietnamese temple in Kushinagar

Figure: Japanese temple in Kushinagar

5.7 Other Buddhist temples in Kushinagar

There are multiple Buddhist monasteries built by the governments or devotees from different Buddhist countries. These include the Thai monastery, Burmese monastery, Japanese temple and other temples.

5.8 Conclusion

In this chapter, we have discussed Kushinagar, the site of the parinirvana stupa and the place where the Buddha passed away into Nirvana.

Chapter 6: Sarnath, site of Buddha's first sermon

Sarnath is one of the four primary sites of Buddhist pilgrimage and located close to the famous holy city of Varanasi. It is the site of the first sermon of Dhammachakkapavattana sutta or Sutra of turning of wheel of dharma.

Figure: Map showing location of Sarnath in Uttar Pradesh state in north India. Latitude: 25.3815° N, Longitude: 83.0218° E

Location & Access

Latitude: 25.3815° N, Longitude: 83.0218° E

Nearest Airport: Varanasi (Lal Bahadur Shastri) Airport, approx. 30 km.

By shared auto or taxi from Varanasi Cantonment railway station (approx. 9 km).

Best time to visit: October to March.

6.1 How to reach Sarnath

Sarnath is only 9 km from Varanasi and the ghats of the river Ganga. Varanasi is well connected by air, rail and roads. Varanasi airport is the nearest airport. To reach Sarnath from Varanasi city, one can take a taxi or a shared auto. Or else, one can directly reach Sarnath from Varanasi airport.

To reach Sarnath from Varanasi city, one can take a shared or reserved auto or taxi from Varanasi Cantonment railway station to Pahariya, Asapur that goes to Sarnath. The journey by shared auto takes 1 hour, around 9 km from Varanasi to Sarnath. Taking a taxi is much faster, depending on the traffic.

Figure: Dhammekh stupa in Sarnath

Figure: Ashoka pillar in Sarnath archeological complex

Figure: Ruins of Mulagandha kuti vihara in Sarnath

Figure: Ruins of other temples in Sarnath

Figure: Ruins of other temples in Sarnath

6.2 Sarnath archeological complex

This is part of the archeological site under care of ASI (Archeological survey of India). It is very clean and well maintained.

Visitors have to first buy tickets from the nearby ASI ticket office to visit the complex.

This is a huge complex and includes the following:

- **Dhamekh stupa**: this is a huge imposing stupa built by king Ashoka. There are Mauryan or Gupta era decorations on all the sides. It is quite an imposing structure. Many Buddhist pilgrims circumambulate and chant suttas around this stupa. Others quietly meditate. It does get pretty hot during the summer months.

- Ruins of 8 monasteries, one built by the queen of the Garhwala king in 12th century. This includes the ancient **Mulagandha kuti stupa**, where the Buddha stayed. It also has ruins of the place where buddha used to do walking meditation, a temple called **Pancha ayatana temple** whose foundations are still visible.

- **Asoka pillar**: This is also part of the excavated site. The top of this asoka pillar became the national emblem of india and got moved to the archeological museum. the script is Brahmi and proclaims that the dhamma shall never get extinguished. This is kept in a glass cabinet so that visitors may not damage it.

- A destroyed stupa, destroyed for building materials in 1794 by the Diwan of the king of Benaras, from where the relics were found and preserved and sometimes displayed at the Mahabodhi temple next door. This stupa was meant to keep the relics.

- Small Votive stupas

- The temple ruins commemorating the place where buddha made the first Dhamma sermon after enlightenment.

It is clean and well preserved by ASI. Many statues found are displayed at the museum nearby.

Figure: Exterior of Sarnath Archeological Museum

6.3 Sarnath archeological museum

This was the first on site museum established by ASI or Archeological Survey of India. it is built in the structure of a Buddhist monastery with a central courtyard and 4 galleries on the sides.

The museum has air conditioning, drinking water facilities, toilets and a small refreshment shop as well as a handicraft shop. Entry fee for Indians is Rs 15 (subject to change), mobile phones and bags to be left in locker at the entrance, keys of locker will be given to you.

The Lion Capital of Ashoka, excavated from Sarnath in the main gallery of the museum, is now the national symbol of India. It has 4 lions symbolizing the fearless declaration of Dharma in all four directions, below that are a cow and bull, below that is an inverted lotus. Behind it was a wheel with 24 spokes, but it was damaged and separated.

The museum also houses the famous standing Buddha in the Gandhara style of meditation. It was built in the 10th century AD under the Gupta kings who patronized Buddhism as well as Hinduism.

The galleries of the museum have articles from Sarnath, sculptures of Hindu deities like Surya etc., Buddhist sculptures of different eras, life of Buddha, Bodhisattva etc. Many objects were loaned to the Palace Museum of China and other museums around the world. The museum also has a section on the importance of the Sarnath Archaeological Site.

Figure: Chaukhandi Stupa in Sarnath

6.4 Chaukhandi Stupa in Sarnath

This is a huge stupa. On top of the stupa is a brick structure built by the Mughals, to commemorate the visit of the Mughal Emperor Akbar to the site.

There is a beautiful garden around the stupa as well.

Figure: Mulagandhakuti Vihara in Sarnath

6.5 Mulagandhakuti Vihara

Mulagandhakuti vihara is run by the Mahabodhi society of India. It was built by the efforts of Angarika dharampala who fought for many ancient Indian buddhist sites to be restored and worshipped.

The Mulagandhakuti vihara complex is situated in a prime location in Sarnath, walking distance from the Dhammekh stupa. It is one of the first things one can see after arriving in sarnath.

Mobile phones must be switched off when inside the temple. One can keep shoes outside for free in the shoe stand.

Inside the temple is a huge statue of the Buddha, a large framed picture of Dharampala and paintings on buddha's life by a japanese artist. There is also a bookshop of Buddhist books by Mahabodhi society in English and Hindi and foreign languages.

Many tour groups keep coming here so gets a little busy sometimes.

Adjacent to the temple is a small zoo. Part of the same complex is a Burmese shrine with the Dhammachakka sutta in different languages besides the bodhi tree, brought back from Sri Lanka and the branch of the same tree taken to Sri Lanka by Mahinda and Sanghamitra, Asoka's children.

There are lots of grounds to sit and relax.

At the entrance are various slogans from the Dhammapada in different languages.

Anagarika Dharampala's statue is also present as a way of remembering his contributions to Buddhism, since he lived, worked and died in Sarnath.

A casket of precious relics was excavated and given to Mahabodhi society, which display them once a year around November. This casket was extracted from the stupa when the divan of king of Banaras accidently destroyed it to extract building materials in 18th century.

Figure: Anagarika Dharampala museum in Sarnath

6.6 Anagarika Dharampala museum in Sarnath

Anagarika Dharamapala was a fearless warrior in the cause of Buddhism, especially in reclaiming and restoring various Buddhist sites in India.

This museum contains photos from the life of Anagarika Dharampala, his visit to the religions conference in New York in 1893, his books and letters, his stay in Sarnath, establishment of Mahabodhi society, the lawsuit about reclaiming Buddhist holy sites which they lost to a mahant, meeting Indian political leaders like Mahatma Gandhi and Jawaharlal Nehru etc. it is an exhibition of the Buddhist revival in India, in fact.

Figure: Interior of Chinese temple in Sarnath

Figure: Tibetan monastery in Sarnath

Figure: Japanese temple in Sarnath

Figure: Japanese peace pagoda in Sarnath

Figure: Burmese temple in Sarnath

6.7 Other temples in Sarnath

Other temples in Sarnath include Tibetan, Chinese, Thai, Burmese monastery, and peace pagoda.

6.8 Conclusion

In this chapter, we have discussed Sarnath, the site where the wheel of Dhamma was set in motion by the Buddha, and the various Buddhist temples and stupas in Sarnath.

Chapter 7: Sravasti, site of Anathapindaka's Grove and Sankissa

In this chapter, we discuss Sravasti, also called Savatthi in Pali language. This is the place where Buddha spent many years of his life in Anathapindika's grove. We also briefly discuss Sankissa, the site where the Buddha is said to have descended from Tushita heaven.

Figure: Map showing location of Sravasti in Uttar Pradesh state in north India. Latitude: 27.5070° N, Longitude: 82.0480° E

Location & Access

Sravasti — Latitude: 27.5070° N, Longitude: 82.0480° E (Uttar Pradesh, India)

Best accessed by taxi or hired car from Lucknow (approx. 3.5 hrs) or Gorakhpur (approx. 2.5 hrs).

Sankissa — Farrukhabad district, UP; best accessed by private vehicle.

7.1 How to get there

Sravasti is in Uttar Pradesh state in North India. It is good to hire a taxi or drive a car from Lucknow. One can also get to Sravasti by car from Gorakhpur.

Figure: Gandhakuti or fragrant hut, site of the Buddha's residence in Jetavana in Sravasti

Figure: Double stupa and bodhi tree in Jetavana in Sravasti

7.2 Jetavana

Jetavana in Shravasti is the place where the Buddha spent most of his life. It originally belonged to a prince named Jeta. It was donated to the Buddha by a wealthy nobleman named Anathapindika, who bought the grove from Prince Jeta.

The site is very clean and beautifully maintained by the Archaeological Survey of India.

It includes the location of the grove of Anathapindika, where the Buddha spent most of his rainy season. It has many temples, votive stupas and monasteries. It has a Bodhi tree where Buddha meditated and a temple at the site of Gandhakuti which was Buddha's hut where he stayed. The grounds are spread over a vast area and include a number of ruins. It is good to meditate near Bodhi tree and Gandhakuti. It is advisable to visit during the winter months, as the weather is more pleasant during that time.

Figure: Angulimala stupa in Sravasti

7.3 Angulimala stupa in sravasti

This stupa is dedicated to Angulimala, the ferocious robber and killer who used to collect human finger sand made a necklace to them, but later became a disciple of the Buddha.

Angulimala stupa is fenced off now, so visitors cannot climb it. It is well preserved. It has a tunnel below it. Bricks of this ancient stupa are from Kushana kingdom era.

Figure: Kacchi kuti Mahet in Sravasti

7.4 Kacchi kuti mahet in Sravasti

Kachhi Kuti Mahet is a well-organized archaeological structure made of bricks. The ruins can be climbed using stairs. One needs to be careful not to trip and fall.

Many Buddhist artefacts were discovered here and taken to museums. It is located right next to the Angulimal Stupa or Pakki Kuti.

Figure: Elephant capital at Sankissa. One of the Pillars of Ashoka, 3rd century BCE. By Author: J. Homany - This file has been extracted from another file, CC BY-SA 2.0, https://commons.wikimedia.org/w/index.php?curid=52578068

7.5 Sankissa

Sankissa, also known as Sankasya or Sankassa, is a lesser-known but profoundly symbolic site. According to Buddhist tradition, the Buddha ascended to the Tushita heaven to teach the Abhidhamma to his mother, and later descended back to earth here, accompanied by Indra and Brahma. The site symbolizes the Buddha's role not just as a teacher of humans, but also as a cosmic teacher to gods. The descent to Sankissa is often depicted in Buddhist art and celebrated as one of the "Eight Great Events" (Ashtamahapratiharya) of the Buddha's life.

How to Get There: Sankissa is located in Farrukhabad district of Uttar Pradesh. The nearest major towns are Farrukhabad (around 50 km away) and Kannauj. It is relatively remote and best accessed by private vehicle or pilgrimage tour.

Main Sites to Visit in Sankissa are as follows:

- Ashokan Pillar Base: The remains of a pillar marking the Buddha's descent from heaven.
- Excavated Monastery Ruins: Foundations of ancient monasteries and stupas.
- Shrine of Descent: A temple marking the site of the Buddha's return from heaven, reconstructed in modern times.

7.6 Conclusion

In this chapter, we have discussed Sravasti, the site of Anathapindaka's grove where the Buddha lived and preached for many years. We have also discussed Sankissa.

Chapter 8: Ajanta and Ellora and other Buddhist caves

In this chapter we discuss some of the principal caves that are related to Buddhism in Maharashtra, namely Ajanta and Ellora caves near Aurangabad, Kanheri caves near Mumbai, and Bojjhanakonda caves near Vishakhapatnam. There are many other Buddhist caves situated all over India.

Figure: Map showing location of Ajanta caves in Maharashtra state in West India. Latitude: 20.5522° N, Longitude: 75.7033° E

Location & Access

Ajanta — Latitude: 20.5522° N, Longitude: 75.7033° E (approx. 105 km from Aurangabad)

Ellora — approx. 35 km from Aurangabad city

Nearest Airport: Aurangabad (Chhatrapati Sambhajinagar) Airport.

Allow a full day for either Ajanta or Ellora; they cannot be visited together in one day.

8.1 How to get there

The closest airport to Ajanta and Ellora caves is Aurangabad, from where one may get a taxi or bus to visit the caves. Ellora caves is much closer to Aurangabad (35 km), while Ajanta is a much father (105 km). It typically takes several hours, probably a full day, to visit either Ajanta or Ellora. Ellora entry fees was Rs 40 for Indians, 600 for foreigners, in 2019, although it might be increased now.

Mumbai airport is the closest one to Kanheri caves, from where one can take a taxi to Sanjay Gandhi National Park or else travel in Mumbai local trains to Borivali station and take an auto, taxi or bus to Sanjay Gandhi national park to see the Kanheri caves. One has to buy separate tickets for entry to Sanjay Gandhi National Park, the shared jeep to take you to the caves and Kanheri caves itself.

For Bojjhanakonda caves, the closest airport is Vizag or Vishakhapatnam, from where one may take a taxi.

Figure: Layout of the Ajanta caves

Figure: One of the richly painted cave temples of Ajanta

*Figure: Famous painting of Bodhisattva Padmapani on the walls of one of
the Ajanta caves*

Figure: Meditation hall in Ajanta caves

Figure: Richly carved entrance to a chaitya hall in one of the Ajanta caves

Figure: Inside of Cave 10 Chaitya in Ajanta

8.2 Ajanta Caves

Ajanta caves are built on a mound, on the side of a hill. Ajanta caves are known for their rich artwork on the walls depicting scenes from the Jatakas, scenes from Buddha's life and statues of various bodhisattvas.

Some of the features of different caves are as follows:

- Cave 1 has rich murals although its a bit dark.
- Cave 2 is a beautiful Mahayana monastery also with rich murals from the Jataka tales
- Caves 9-10 are the oldest (Theravada) chaityas in Ajanta Caves
- 16-17 are very large monasteries
- Cave 19 is the most beautiful and perfect chaitya
- Cave 29 is a richly decorated Chaitya cave

Figure: Richly carved entrance to one of the Buddhist caves at Ellora

Figure: Stupa at one of the Buddhist caves at Ellora

Figure: Three floored monastery. One of the rock cut Buddhist caves at Ellora

8.3 Buddhist Caves at Ellora

The Ellora caves have all three: Hindu, Buddhist and Jain caves. The first 14 caves are Buddhist and are probably the oldest. There are also

Hindu caves and Jain caves, the most famous being the Kalasanathar cave dedicated to the Hindu God Shiva, which is possibly the biggest rock cut temple in the world.

- The earliest cave 1 is simplest. It just has cells for monks to meditate, opening to a small courtyard.
- Cave 10 is a beautiful Buddhist chaitya gruha. It has a large Buddha statue. Atmosphere inside the cave is peaceful. First floor has very beautiful sculptures outside the cave
- One cave is a huge chaitya hall, similar to the ones at Ajanta, it is two storied.
- There were two multi story monasteries with chambers to meditate. 5 Dhyani buddhas and other sculptures were exquisite. Most were Mahayana style buddhas and bodhisattvas, surrounded by gods and heavenly beings.

Figure: One of the Kanheri caves in Borivali National Park in Mumbai

Figure: Rock cut monastery, part of the Kanheri caves in Mumbai

Figure: Richly carved wall, part of the Kanheri caves in Mumbai

8.3 Kanheri caves in Mumbai, Maharashtra

This is a cave complex of more than 100 caves deep inside Sanjay gandhi National Park, on top of a hill 7 km from the entrance to the park. Entry is Rupees 25 for Indians, 300 foreigners (subject to change).

There are lots of monkeys around so be careful with any food you are carrying.

Cave 67, 34, 1, 2, 3 are quite beautiful.

These are all Buddhist caves, roughly dating back to the time of Ajanta and Ellora. The drainage system of the caves is quite impressive. Some of the caves are carved into the rocks, so care must be taken when climbing the rocks to visit them.

Figure: Bojjhanakonda cave near Vishakhapatnam in Andhra Pradesh

8.3 Bojjhana Konda caves near Vishakhapatnam in Andhra Pradesh state

To go from Visakhapatnam city to Bojjana Konda Hill, one has to take bus number 500 from the bus depot called "RTC Complex" in Visakhapatnam. Get off the bus at the nearest town called Anakapalle. Then one has to hire an auto from the bus stop to reach the caves. Otherwise, one can hire a taxi from Visakhapatnam.

Visiting the Bojjanakonda site is free. One has to climb stairs till Bojjhana Konda hill. There is a main cave, and statues of Buddha and Bodhisattva are carved on the cave. Inside there is a stupa surrounded by pillars. The nave has two levels, with another carving and a nave above. There is another way to go further up, stairs are needed to climb there. On that way there is a huge monastic complex with cells for the monks. It can also be climbed and there is also a temple here. There is another huge stupa in front.

8.4 Other Caves

There are a number of other Buddhist caves across the length and breadth of India. Some of the notable ones include:

- Bhaja and Karla caves near Lonawala in Maharashtra
- Pandavleni or Nasik caves in Nashik, Maharashtra
- Bedse and Junnar caves in Pune, Maharashtra
- Dhamnar caves in Madhya Pradesh
- Pitalkhora and Ghatotkacha caves in Aurangabad, Maharashtra, as well as Aurangabad caves
- Bagh caves in Dhar in Madhya Pradesh
- Barabar caves in Bihar
- Guntupalli caves in West Godavari district of Andhra Pradesh

8.5 Conclusion

In this chapter, we have discussed a few important Buddhist caves starting from Ajanta and Ellora caves in Maharashtra near Aurangabad, Kanheri caves in Mumbai and Bojjhanakonda cave near Vishakhapatnam in Andhra Pradesh.

Chapter 9: Rajgir, site of Vulture's Peak

In this chapter we discuss Rajgir, the ancient capital of the Magadha kingdom and where Buddha stayed many years and spoke the heart sutra and many other Mahayana sutras.

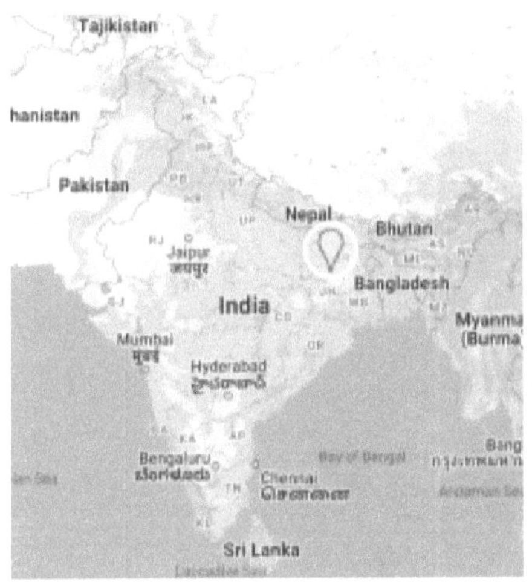

Figure: Location of Rajgir in Bihar state in north India. Latitude: 25.0056° N, Longitude: 85.4219° E

Location & Access

Latitude: 25.0056° N, Longitude: 85.4219° E

Easily reached by bus or taxi from Bodhgaya (approx. 80 km) or Nalanda (approx. 15 km).

Best time to visit: October to March.

9.1 How to get there

Rajgir is located in Bihar state. It can be easily accessed by bus or car/ taxi from Bodh Gaya.

Figure: Vulture's Peak in Rajgir

Figure: Vietnamese pilgrims at Vulture's peak in Rajgir

Figure: View of sunrise in Vulture's peak in Rajgir

Figure: Shariputra's cave near vulture's peak in Rajgir. Shariputra or Sariputta was one of the chief students of the Buddha, skilled in meditation.

9.2 Vulture's peak or Gridhrakuta

Vulture Peak is the place where Buddha spoke the Heart Sutra and other Mahayana Sutras. It is shaped like a vulture's beak, hence the name.

It takes about half an hour to climb the hill to the summit. On the way there are the Sariputra and Maudgalyana caves and the ruins of a monastery. On the summit is the seat of the Buddha and the seat of his chief disciple Ananda. It is a wonderful place to meditate. Visitors can clean and offer flowers to the shrine at the top, as well as sit and meditate

Figure: Entrance to the Saptapani cave in Rajgir, site of the first buddhist council

9.2 Saptaparni cave

This is the historical site where the first Buddhist Council was held soon after the death of the Buddha. The caves are very dark, and the entrance is quite narrow. Visitors should be wary of bats.

Figure: World peace stupa (Vishwa shanti stupa) near vulture's peak in Rajgir

Figure: Lake in Venu Van in Rajgir, a beautiful garden where Buddha used to stay.

9.3 Venu Van

It is an ancient site where Buddha meditated. Now this place has been converted into a beautiful natural park. It also has a lake, which marks the spot where Buddha used to walk and meditate.

9.4 Conclusion

In this chapter we have discussed a few of the historical Buddhist sites in Rajgir in Bihar, ancient capital of the Magadha empire.

Chapter 10: Sanchi Stupa: the model stupa built by Ashoka

In this chapter we discuss the Sanchi stupa, which was built by emperor Ashoka and which formed the model of most subsequent Buddhist stupas.

Figure: Location of Sanchi stupa near Bhopal in Madhya Pradesh state in central India. Latitude: 23.4793° N, Longitude: 77.7391° E

Location & Access

Latitude: 23.4793° N, Longitude: 77.7391° E

Located 46 km northeast of Bhopal, Madhya Pradesh.

Bhopal is well connected by rail and air. Taxi or bus from Bhopal to Sanchi.

Open sunrise to sunset. Arrive well before 4:30 pm.

10.1 How to get there

Sanchi stupa is located at Sanchi, close to Bhopal, the capital of Madhya Pradesh state in central India. Bhopal can be accessed through flights from major cities such as Delhi, or by road or rail.

Figure: Richly carved gate of the Sanchi stupa

Figure: Exterior view of the Sanchi stupa

Figure: Gupta era temple next to Sanchi stupa

10.2 Sanchi Stupa

The stupa of Sanchi is built over a vast area. It is on the top of the hill and is open only from sunrise to sunset. Visitors should make sure that they reach before 4:30 pm so that they can see all the sights of the complex properly.

The Great Stupa (Stupa No. 1) is the crown jewel of Sanchi. Emperor Ashoka built the original hemispherical stupa over relics of the Buddha; it was later enlarged to its present size during the Shunga period (2nd–1st century BCE). Its four toranas (gateways), the finest examples of early Buddhist relief sculpture in India, depict scenes from the Buddha's life and the Jataka tales in extraordinary detail.

The Buddha is represented symbolically (by a wheel, footprints, an empty throne) rather than in human form, reflecting early aniconic Buddhist art. The complex spreads over a large hilltop area and includes numerous other stupas, temples and monastery remains from the

Maurya, Shunga, Satavahana and Gupta periods. The 5th-century Gupta Temple (Temple 17), a flat-roofed stone structure with a colonnaded porch, is almost perfectly preserved and houses Buddha images in the Mahayana style.

The complex has many monasteries, many stupas and temples from different eras like Gupta and Maurya. The main stupa has amazing carvings. It is circular in shape. It has richly carved gates on all four sides.

An important place in the complex of Sanchi is the Gupta temple. The temple is largely intact. Inside it there are statues of Buddha in Mahayana style.

The cost of an entry ticket to Sanchi Stupa is Rs 40 for Indians and SAARC nationals, again subject to change, and is higher for other foreigners.

Figure: Theravada temple with relics, next to Sanchi stupa

10.3 Theravada temple with relics (Mahabodhi Society)

A Mahabodhi Society temple situated just outside the main Sanchi complex houses the relics of Sariputra and Maudgalyayana, the two chief disciples of the Buddha, originally discovered at Sanchi. The relics are displayed to the public on a few occasions each year.

10.4 Sanchi Museum

The ASI Museum at Sanchi displays many of the original sculptural elements from the stupas and gateways, providing context for what one sees in the main complex. Well worth visiting before or after the main site.

10.5 Conclusion

In this chapter, we have discussed the Sanchi stupa built by emperor Ashoka.

Chapter 11: Amarawati Stupa, with amazing marbles

In this chapter, we discuss Amarawati Stupa, which is a very famous stupa. Amarawati stupa is located near Guntur in Andhra Pradesh state in South India.

Figure: Map showing location of Amarawati in Andhra Pradesh state in south India. Latitude: 16.5726° N, Longitude: 80.3578° E

Location & Access

Latitude: 16.5726° N, Longitude: 80.3578° E

Nearest major cities: Vijayawada and Guntur (approx. 60 km).

By bus from Vijayawada bus station (Bus 301 to Amaravati), or from Guntur bus station.

11.1 How to get there

To get there, go to the city of Guntur or Vijaywada by bus from Hyderabad, then take 301 bus from Vijaywada to Amarawati. Guntur bus station too has several buses that go to Amarawati.

Figure: Richly carved marbles (built out of limestone) in front of Amarawati stupa

Figure: Ruins of Amarawati stupa

11.2 Mahastupa at Amarawati

Although the present state of the stupa is in ruins and most of its marble has been removed and displayed in the British Museum and other museums in London, we can still see and admire the glory of the stupa's heyday.

The marbles of the Amaravati Stupa depict 91 various scenes from the life of the Buddha and the Jatakas. Some of the marbles are on display in the Government Museum, Chennai, which are discussed later in this book.

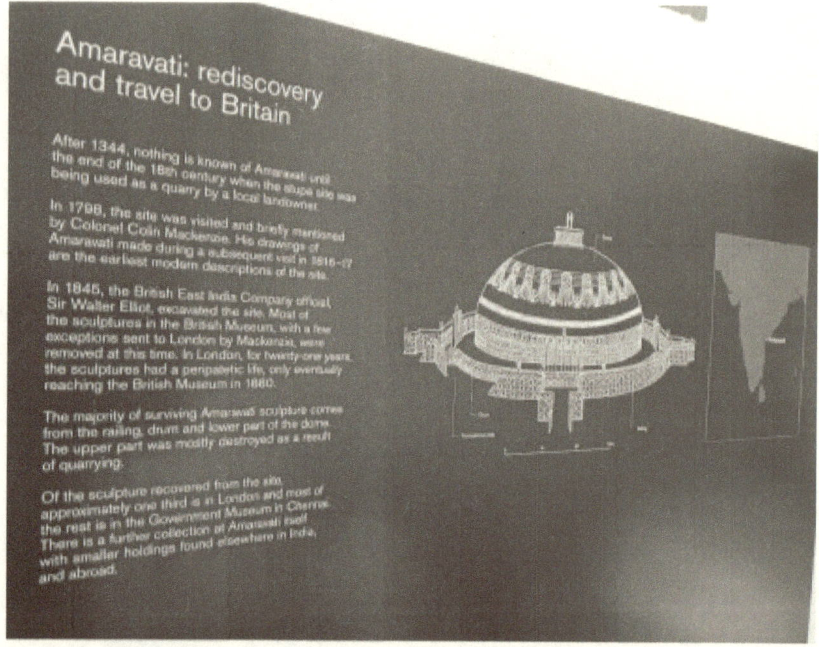

Figure: Amarawati marbles section in the British Museum in London

Today, the site of Amaravati Stupa consists of some sculptures and the mound where the original Stupa was located with all its remains.

The Archaeological Museum of Amaravati includes a scale model of the stupa in 3D, several stupa stones related to the life of the Buddha, several Bodhisattva sculptures taken from Amaravati and surrounding sites.

The local Andhra Pradesh state government wants to promote this place for Buddhist tourism, so the infrastructure is improving.

11.3 Archeological survey museum in Amarawati

The Archaeological Survey of India (ASI) museum in Amaravati is quite informative. It displays various Buddhist artefacts including Amaravati and gives a brief history of Buddhism in the region. The museum opens at 10 am but the Amaravati ruins site is open from 9 am onwards. Cost for Indians is Rs 25 (subject to change). No photos are allowed inside the museum.

11.4 Conclusion

In this chapter, we have discussed the mahastupa at Amarawati, which at one time is said to be the largest stupa in South India.

Chapter 12: Nagarjunakonda hill, site of the displaced and recreated stupas

In this chapter, we discuss the Buddhist site of Nagarjunakonda. It has various important Buddhist historical artifacts. Unfortunately, most of the place was submerged by construction of the Nagarjunasagar dam on the Krishna river in the 1960s. However archeologists rescued many Buddhist artifacts and they can be viewed on an island on top of a hill in the lake created by the dam, which can be reached by boat from the mainland.

Figure: Location of Nagarjunakonda in Andhra Pradesh in South India. Latitude: 16.2335° N, Longitude: 79.2510° E

Location & Access

Latitude: 16.2335° N, Longitude: 79.2510° E

Nearest city: Hyderabad (approx. 4 hrs by road). Drive to Nagarjunasagar township.

Ferry to the island departs around 9:30 am; last return boat approx. 2:30 pm.

12.1 How to get there

To get to Nagarjunakonda, we can drive a car or taxi from Hyderabad city to the Nagarjunakonda ferry launch station, and from there take a ferry to the island.

Ferry service is available to the island from both Macherla in Andhra Pradesh state as well as from Telangana state.

By public transport from Hyderabad, one can take a bus from Hyderabad MGBS bus station to Macherla town, the journey takes 4 hours. Then one has to take another bus from Macherla town bus stop for a distance of 30 km from Macherla to Nagarjunasagar township, which will cost Rs 30. The bus drops one on the Andhra Pradesh side of the dam. It seems that the river Krishna is the boundary between the states. From there, one can take a shared auto or a reserved auto from the bus drop location to the township.

The first boat to Nagarjunakonda Island is at 9:30 AM, although sometimes it can be delayed till 10:30 AM. A ferry ticket costs 150 rupees, and the museum on the island also has separate tickets. Everyone on the ferry gets a life jacket.

Figure: Guide map of Nagarjunakonda island

Figure: Boat from the mainland to Nagarjunakonda

Figure: Standing Buddha statue in Nagarjunakonda

Figure: Sinhalese vihara at Nagarjunakonda

Figure: Sinhalese vihara at Nagarjunakonda

Figure: Reconstructed Mahastupa at Nagarjunakonda

Figure: Temple next to the Mahastupa

Figure: Bodhisri Chaitya at Nagarjunakonda

Figure: Ancient huge tank built by the Iksvaku kings, with a stairway leading into the tank

Figure: Standing Buddha inside the Nagarjunakonda site museum and entrance to the museum

12.2 Recreated Buddhist structures on Nagarjunakonda island

The structures on the Nagarjunakonda island include a museum and other structures.

- Museum: The Archaeological Survey of India Museum can be seen first on Nagarjunakonda Island. It has a wonderful collection of stone sculptures from the 3rd century Ikshvaku dynasty with scenes from the life of Buddha. Additionally, it has a section on sculptures from the region. Many structures were submerged when the Nagarjunasagar Dam was built on the Krishna River in the 1960s. In addition to the museum, the island has renovated Buddhist temples and monasteries. These include the following:
- A huge and deep tank built by the Iksvaku kings. The water inside the tank is said to be holy.
- A megalithic burial ground.
- A beautiful Sinhalese (Sri Lankan) monastery including a standing Buddha image and stupa.
- The mahastupa, which is the main highlight of the island. It was the principal stupa of the Krishna valley, having a bone relic of the Buddha. Dalai lama and many senior Tibetan lamas and monks have planted trees and made stone and scarf offerings near the maha stupa.
- There is also an aswamedha horse sacrifice bath.

Finally, after seeing the sites on the island, one can take the boat back from the island after an hour, or wait for the next boat. One should be careful to leave the island before to last boat at 2:30 pm or so.

Figure: Reconstructed university complex at Anupu with moonstone

Figure: Monastery ruins at Anupu

Figure: Reconstructed ampitheatre in Anupu

12.3 Anupu Nagarjuna Sagar

After visiting the island of Nagarjunakonda, one can hire an auto and go to Anupu, which is about 7 km from the launch station.

Some monasteries have been rebuilt in Anupu. It consists of a huge monastic complex and university campus. One part of it had a wonderful moonstone. Another construction at Anupu is a huge ancient amphitheater made of stone bricks

Figure: The Nagarjunsagar dam, due to which these areas became submerged in 1960s

Figure: The main stupa at Buddhavanam

Figure: Buddhavanam museum

Figure: Richly carved scenes from Buddha's life on the walls of the main stupa at Buddhavanam

Figure: Meditation hall on the first floor of the main stupa at Buddhavanam

Figure: Statue of Buddha teaching disciples in the park at Buddhavanam

12.4 Buddhavanam

Buddhavanam is a new site built by the Telangana state government, which is like a Buddhist theme park. This includes the following:

- A massive two-storey curved stupa with a large seating area for meditation
- A small Buddhist museum
- A park having six zones on different Buddhist themes such as Jataka tales, scenes from the life of Buddha, teachings of Buddhism, Stupa architecture in different countries and others.

Buddhavanam is walking distance from the boat launch station for Nagarjunakonda.

12.4 Conclusion

In this chapter we have discussed important Buddhist ruins found at Nagarjunakonda, that were displaced and recreated because of the construction of a dam in 1960s.

Chapter 13: Udayagiri, Ratnagiri and Lalitagiri monasteries in Odisha

In this chapter, we discuss a few important Buddhist sites in Odisha state in east India, including the Mahayana Buddhist monastery complexes of Udayagiri, Ratnagiri and Lalitagiri.

Figure: Location of Ratnagiri in Odisha state in east India. Latitude: 20.6236° N, Longitude: 86.5570° E

Location & Access

Ratnagiri — Latitude: 20.6236° N, Longitude: 86.5570° E

Approx. 100 km from Bhubaneswar on NH-16/NH-5A (toward Paradip).

Best as a day trip by taxi from Bhubaneswar.

Follow the blue signs to the Buddhist monasteries.

13.1 How to get there

One can see the three complexes, Udayagiri, Ratnagiri and Lalitgiri from Bhubaneshwar, the capital of Odisha state, on a day trip costing

Rs 3100 on taxi in 2018 (subject to change). It is about 2 hours from bhubaneshwar, 100 km, first go towards Cuttack on NH5 and then take NH5A national highway towards Paradip port. Follow the blue signs towards the buddhist monasteries.

Figure: Main entrance to Ratnagiri monastery

Figure: Buddha head and artifacts in Ratnagiri monastery

Figure: Shrines in Ratnagiri monastery

Figure: Votive stupas in Ratnagiri monastery

Figure: Main monastery building in Ratnagiri

13.2 Ratnagiri monastery

Ratnagiri is a Vajrayana monastery. ASI maintains it. Entry fees is Rs 15 for Indians, subject to change.

Ratnagiri ('Hill of Gems') is named for the distinctive greenish and reddish gemstone-bearing rock from which its monastery doorways and fittings were made. It is believed to have been part of the Lalitagiri university complex. Entry fees are modest (Indians: approx. Rs. 15). The complex includes at least four monasteries. The main monastery is a large and beautiful structure with more than 15 monk chambers and remarkable Buddha statues. The second, smaller monastery stands adjacent. An impressive collection of votive stupas of different Buddhist deities is also preserved here. The main stupa complex, one large stupa surrounded by smaller ones, occupies a grassy area where livestock now graze. The Mahakal Temple, architecturally similar to later Odishan Hindu temples, is also within the site.

Ratnagiri monastery has the following places to see:

- **Main monastery**: There are at least 4 different monasteries at this place. The main monastery is huge and beautiful. There are more than 15 monk chambers where monks used to live and meditate. The Buddha statues in the monastery are amazingly beautiful. There are many different Buddhas. You can climb up and see the monastery walking across the rooftops, but be careful as some of the walls are crumbling.

- **Second monastery**: This is just next to the main monastery, it is a smaller one and simpler as well.
- **Votive stupas**: There is a huge collection of neatly kept stupas of different buddhist dieties, is is possible they were donated to ASI by nearby villagers.
- **Main stupa and smaller stupas**: There is a complex of one big and many smaller stupas. Many cows and goats now graze the area.
- **Mahakal temple**: It is architecturally similar to the later era Hindu temples of Odisha.

Figure: Stupa complex with cluster of stupas at Lalitagiri

Figure: 8th century monastery in Lalitagiri

Figure: Mahastupa at Lalitagiri

13.3 Lalitagiri monastery

The Lalitagiri monastery complex, comprising mainly Mahayana monasteries, is maintained by the ASI archeological survey of India. It was constructed from the 8th to 11th century AD.

It is the largest of the three complexes and contains at least 44 monastery ruins with monks' quarters, hallways and shrines. The principal feature is a great mahastupa on a hill, affording panoramic views of the surrounding countryside. A large cluster of excavated stupas (in varying states of preservation) occupies another area of the site.

Entry fees is Rs 30 for indians, 200 for foreigners, subject to change. It is located close to the main highway. The local state government of Odisha is trying to make it attractive for Buddhist tourists by making good roads and proper facilities.

Figure: Richly decorated shrine in Udayagiri

Figure: Buddha statue inside the shrine in Udayagiri

Figure: Udayagiri monastery stupa

13.4 Udayagiri monastery

Udayagiri ('Hill of the Rising Sun') is a mahayana monastery, built and developed between the 8th and 11th century AD. There is also an incompletely excavated grassy field, which probably needs to be excavated more to get more artifacts.

Udayagiri is also maintained by ASI, entry is free. The surroundings are very clean and beautiful, some cows and goats are roaming the grounds from time to time. The hills and the clear sky and the grassy plains are very pretty.

The main excavated ruins consist of a well preserved stupa with Dhyani buddhas in the 4 directions, as well as a monastery with a well kept shrine. Thanks to ASI the structures have been very well restored. In the monastery, one can see lots of quarters for the monks.

Figure: Shanti stupa at Dhauli

Figure: Daya river, on the bank's of which the Kalinga war was fought, as seen from Dhauli Shanti stupa. It is said to have run red with blood.

13.5 Shanti stupa (peace stupa) at Dhauli hill

This stupa was built by a Japanese group on the Dhauli hill, which was the site of the bloody battle with the Kalingas that convinced emperor Ashoka to become a Buddhist and give up war. It is a huge circular stupa and has statues and images from Buddha's life on four sides of the stupa.

There is also a rock with inscriptions of Emperor Ashoka nearby.

13.6 Conclusion

In this chapter, we have discussed important Buddhist monasteries in Odisha state in east India, including Ratnagiri, Lalitagiri and Udayagiri. We have also discussed the Shanti Stupa at Dhauli hill, site of Kalinga war and emperor Ashoka's conversion to Buddhism.

Chapter 14: Nalanda university complex and Vaishali, site of the second Buddhist council

In this chapter, we discuss the Nalanda university in Bihar state in north India. It was the biggest and most famous of the ancient Buddhist universities and a model for many others. We also discuss Vaishali, which was an important Buddhist site and location of the second Buddhist council after Rajgir.

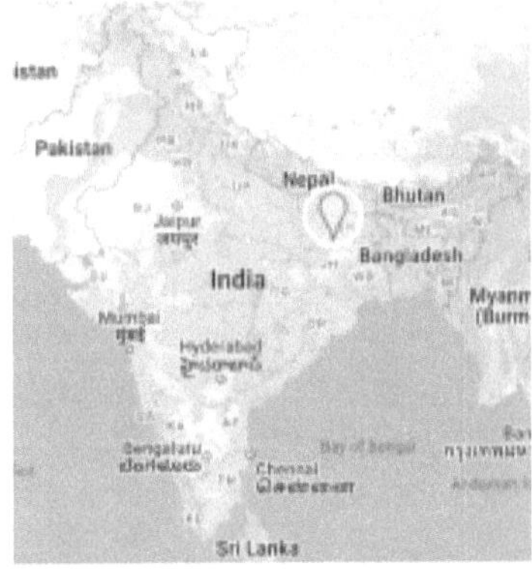

Figure: Location of Nalanda monastery ruins in Bihar state in north India. Latitude: 25.1368° N, Longitude: 85.4432° E

Location & Access

Nalanda — Latitude: 25.1368° N, Longitude: 85.4432° E (Bihar)

Nalanda is 15 km from Rajgir and 85 km from Bodhgaya. Best reached by hired taxi.

Vaishali — Approx. 40 km from Patna, 80 km from Nalanda. Day trip by taxi.

14.1 How to get there

Nalanda university is located in Bihar state, not too far from Rajgir (15 km) and Bodh Gaya (85 km). It is best to hire a private taxi from Bodhgaya or Rajgir to visit Nalanda.

Figure: Temple ruins at Nalanda

Figure: One of the monasteries at Nalanda

Figure: Nalanda ruins with the group kitchen for students

Figure: Temple ruins in Nalanda

Figure: Student room with drainage system

Figure: Stupa at Nalanda

14.2 Ruins of Nalanda university

Nalanda university complex is a UNESCO world heritage site.

The ruins of the ancient university of Nalanda include at least 19 monastic complexes where students stayed and studied. It also has about 12 temples. To avoid harm from visiting tourists, it is not allowed to go close to the temples in Nalanda. However, tourists can visit the student monasteries at Nalanda without any hindrance.

The Nalanda Archaeological Museum is located near the Nalanda Math complex. It houses a number of Buddha and Bodhisattva sculptures excavated from the Nalanda ruins. It is good to go there first to get some context about Nalanda and to see some of the artefacts.

We can hire a guide for a few hundred rupees or as a group.

Nalanda has two main corridors: one for the monasteries and one for the temples. It is said that it had 108 temples in its heyday, but now only 11 monasteries and 11 temples survive. The rest are in mounds below the surrounding villages which have not yet been excavated.

The Nalanda monastery is supposed to be established by the Gupta King Kumaragupta 1 in the 5th century and subsequently enlarged and supported by a variety of patrons, in particular the Pala kings of Bengal. It is said to have been attacked and burnt by the Turkish general Bakhtiyar Khilji in the 13th century, although some accounts also quote a Tibetan source Taranatha which states a dispute with some Brahmins leading to damage to the university's library. Anyway, as per an on-site guide's account, the monastery was reportedly kept burning for six months, even today we can see black ash marks on some of the walls due to burning for six months. Most of the temples were destroyed, but some ruins are still visible, but many monasteries still survive in good condition and can be visited.

The kitchen of the main Nalanda University campus has a granary with a huge brick cooking stove. Some stones glow when light is cast on them, so they are not ordinary stones. The doors and roof were made of wood, so have not survived to this day. Only the brick walls have mainly survived. Each monastery had a courtyard where lectures were given to student monks. It had stone pillars, whose base still exists today.

Nalanda was built over a few centuries under kings from different dynasties. The bricks of the Gupta dynasty are thick, while the bricks of the Pala dynasty are relatively thin. Even today we can see the layers of construction of the monasteries.

The buildings of the monastery are of 2 to 3 floors. The general structure of each monastery is similar. There is an open courtyard, rooms for monks' dormitories, kitchen, granary etc. The revenue from twelve surrounding villages paid for the maintenance of the monastery. The kings made it tax free.

The temples of Nalanda University include Vajrayana (Tantric) temples as well as Mahayana. Pali, Sanskrit, logic, crafts like sculpture, medicine and other sciences were all taught in the university. For prospective students, a difficult entrance test had to be passed by answering correctly several questions asked by the gatekeepers. Students came from all over the world, such as China and Southeast Asia and India. All the professors of Nalanda were expert in their respective fields

Figure: Black Buddha statue next to Nalanda university complex

14.3 Black Buddha statue near Nalanda university

The black buddha statue is said to be one of the shrines in nalanda university that was saved from destruction. Nowadays, it is the subject of a court case It is being worshipped in a small shrine just outside the nalanda university campus.

Figure: Xuanzang memorial at Nalanda

14.4 Xuanzang (Huien Tsang) memorial at Nalanda

Hiuen Tsang Memorial is about 2 km from the Nalanda University ruins site. It is dedicated to the Chinese monk, traveler and translator Hiuen Tsang, who lived in the 7th century AD. He traveled thousands of miles from China under difficult conditions to come to India and study the Buddhist sutras, stayed for many years, carefully recording all his experiences and finally going back to China to share the knowledge. Today, his works provide us with valuable information about Buddhist India of those days. The memorial includes the following:

- A very interesting museum and exhibition about Indian buddhism and contributions from Xuanzhang

- A bell inscribed with the Heart Sutra in Sanskrit and Chinese
- A memorial hall with a shrine to xuanzhang and an exhibition
- The books of Xuanzhang in chinese
- A statue of xuanzhang
- Maps of his travels
- A chinese style traditional epitaph
- In the back side, some structures in Hindi showing the culture etc as Xuanzhang discovered at that time in India

Entry to the memorial is Rs 20 (subject to change).

Figure: Relics stupa at Vaishali. By Amaan Imam - Own work, CC BY-SA 4.0, https://commons.wikimedia.org/w/index.php?curid=73211712

14.5 Vaishali, site of the second Buddhist council

Vaishali is an ancient city of great importance in Buddhist history. It was the capital of the Vajji republic and home to the Lichchavi clan, known for their deep support of the Buddha. The Buddha visited Vaishali several times, and it is believed that he gave his last sermon here before traveling to Kushinagar for his final passing. Vaishali is traditionally believed to be the location of the Second Buddhist

Council, held about a century after the Buddha's parinirvana. It is also the place where Ambapali, a renowned courtesan, offered her mango grove to the Buddha and became a nun.

How to Get There: Vaishali is located in Bihar, around 40 km from Patna and 80 km from Nalanda. It can be visited as a day trip from either Patna or Nalanda via car or taxi.

Main Sites to Visit in Vaishali are as follows:

- Ashokan Pillar: A well-preserved lion capital stands here, commemorating the Buddha's visits.
- Vishali Stupa: Believed to enshrine the Buddha's relics distributed after his cremation.
- Kutagarasala Vihara: A monastery built for the Buddha during his visits; now visible as archaeological ruins.
- Ananda Stupa: Dedicated to the Buddha's attendant Ananda, who died here according to some traditions.

14.6 Conclusion

In this chapter, we have discussed Nalanda, site of the ancient famous university. We have also discussed Vaishali

Chapter 15: Nagpur Deekshabhumi, site of Babasaheb Ambedkar's conversion

In this chapter, we discuss the Deekshabhumi at Nagpur. This was the site where Babasaheb Dr. Bhim Rao Ambedkar, the architect of the constitution of India, converted to Buddhism along with about 600000 followers in the 1950s. Today, Ambedkar Buddhists, also callled Navayana Buddhists, make up most of the Buddhist population of India.

Figure: Location of Deekshabhumi in Nagpur in Central India. Latitude: 21.1317° N, Longitude: 79.0717° E

Location & Access

Latitude: 21.1317° N, Longitude: 79.0717° E

Nagpur is well connected by air, rail and road from major Indian cities.

From Nagpur airport or railway station, take a taxi or auto to Deekshabhumi.

15.1 How to get to Deekshabhumi

Nagpur is located in the state of Maharashtra. Geographically it is the centermost point of India. It is easily reachable by flights from Mumbai,

Delhi, Bangalore and other major cities. From the Nagpur airport, one can take a taxi or auto to Deekshabhumi.

Figure: Deekshabhumi stupa from outside.

Figure: Bodhi tree at Deekshabhumi

Figure: Relics of the Buddha kept inside Deekshabhumi stupa

Figure: Photo exhibition from Babasaheb Dr. BR Ambedkar's life inside Deekshabhumi stupa

15.2 Visiting the site of Deekshabhumi

Today, the site complex contains a huge stupa and museum exhibition, bookstall, and library at the site today.

One needs to deposit one's shoes and large bags before entering the Deekshabhumi stupa.

There are buddha's relics inside the stupa. One can circumambulate the stupa in clockwise direction, offer respects and worship or sit and meditate peacefully inside.

There is an exhibition of photographs from Ambedkar's life inside the stupa.

It is overall a very peaceful and inspiring place.

Figure: Plaque containing the 22 vows of Ambedkar Buddhists at Deekshabhumi

Outside the stupa there is a plaque containing the 22 vows of Ambedkar Buddhists, statues of the Buddha and babasaheb, and a copy of the preamble of the constitution of India.

There is a good bookshop with books in Marathi, English and other languages as well as Buddha statues.

There is also a Bodhi tree on the Deekshabhumi campus. Other things on the campus include a place to stay for bhikshus, a college and office of the Ambedkar memorial organization.

Figure: Dr. Amebedkar Chaityabhumi in Dadar in Mumbai

15.3 Other important places for Ambedkar Buddhists: Chaityabhumi at Dadar

Another important place to visit for Ambedkar Buddhists and those interested in Ambedkar Buddhism is the Dr. Ambedkar memorial and Chaityabhumi at Dadar in Mumbai, where Dr. Ambedkar's samadhi is maintained and his mortal remains are kept.

One can access the Chaityabhumi by taking a Mumbai local train the Dadar railway station and taking an auto or bus from there.

There are many Buddhist books and articles shops near the site. One can quietly visit the stupa and pay one's respects to the samadhi of Dr. Ambedkar. Entry is free.

Figure: BR Ambedkar national memorial in New Delhi

15.4 BR Ambedkar National Memorial in New Delhi

The BR Ambedkar National Memorial in New Delhi, next to the Delhi Vidhan Sabha, is shaped like an open book. Inside are a Bodhi tree, an exhibition of events from Dr. Ambedkar's life, his speeches and writings, a 3D animated statue, and sections on the Indian Constitution and on the Buddha and Buddhism. It is a worthwhile visit for anyone interested in Ambedkar's legacy.

15.5 Conclusion

In this chapter, we have discussed Deekshabhumi at Nagpur and a few other important sites for Ambedkar Buddhists.

Chapter 16: Global Vipassana Pagoda at Mumbai

In this chapter, we discuss the Global Vipassana Pagoda in Mumbai. It was built by Satya Narayan Goenka, the master of Vipassana meditation in India. Goenkaji learned Vipassana meditation from his teacher Sayagi U Ba Khin, who was a student of Vebu Sayadaw, a renowned veteran Buddhist monk and scholar from Myanmar/Burma. Goenkaji brought Vipassana meditation to India and opened several 10-day Vipassana retreat centers in India and abroad.

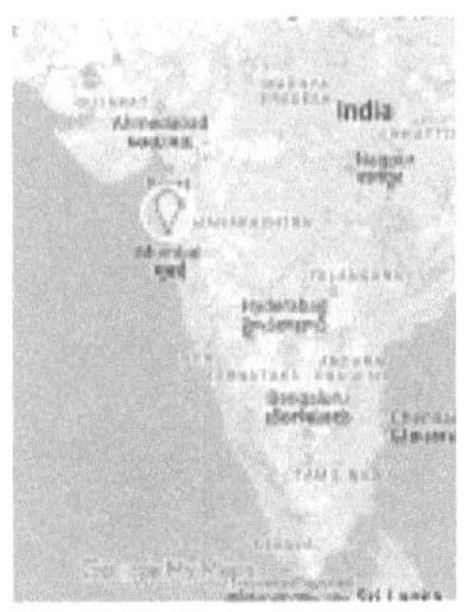

Figure: Location of Global Vipassana Pagoda in Mumbai. Latitude: 19.2284° N, Longitude: 72.8055° E

Location & Access

Latitude: 19.2284° N, Longitude: 72.8055° E

Train to Borivali (Western Railway), then Bus 247 or auto to Gorai Creek.

Ferry from Essel World Jetty to the pagoda (approx. 20 min).

Open 9 am to 5:30 pm. Free entry. Security check at entrance.

16.1 How to get to Global Vipassana Pagoda

To reach the Global Vipassana Pagoda, one needs to take a Mumbai local train from Andheri to Borivali. From the Borivali station, one can take a 247 bus from Borivali station to Gorai Creek or Gorai Khadi. Or else one can take an auto. From Gorai creek one needs to buy a return ticket for the Essel world Jetty (Rs 70 return, subject to change). The ferry reaches the pagoda in 20 minutes. Then one needs to take a short walk to reach the Global Vipassana pagoda. One needs to go back the same way, back to the Gorai creek via the Essel world ferry service.

The pagoda is free and open from 9 am till 5:30 pm. There is a security check before entering, one can install an app called "Global Vipassana Pagoda" on Android or iphone app store which gives a guided audio tour of the pagoda.

Figure: Global Vipassana Pagoda in Mumbai

Figure: Buddha statue and meditation bell in Global Vipassana Pagoda campus

16.2 Global Vipassana Pagoda campus

The Global Vipassana Pagoda is huge, almost as big as the famous Shwedagon Pagoda in Yangon. It is built in the traditional Burmese style, with doors of Burmese teak, marble donated from Myanmar for the circumambulation path. It is golden in color and has the relics of Buddha inside it.

Inside is a vast meditation hall capable of accommodating around 8,000 meditators. The atmosphere is deeply peaceful. Only experienced meditators who have completed a 10-day Vipassana retreat are permitted to meditate inside; other visitors may observe from a viewing gallery in complete silence.

The Global Vipassana Pagoda is built in the traditional Burmese style. Its doors are made of Burmese teak wood, the marble for the circumambulation has also been donated from Burma. There is a magnificent Burmese style entrance gate, a shrine for 5 deities near the water fountain, a bell which is surrounded by Burmese style deities or Dwarapalas.

Those interested can take a free 10-minute guided Anapana breathing meditation session in Goenkaji's recorded voice in a nearby hall.

There is also a gallery of Buddhist art, which has scenes from the life of the Buddha with explanations. Audio guides are also available. There is also a film show on Goenkaji and how Vipassana spread in India. All around the pagoda, there are posters about the history of the pagoda, Vipassana and science, Vipassana in schools and prisons, etc.

There is also a shop selling Sayagyi U Ba Khin books, Goenkaji books and some simple souvenirs. There is also a separate hall in the adjacent building for those doing Vipassana meditation retreats for 10 days and above

A downloadable audio guide app ('Global Vipassana Pagoda') is available for both Android and iPhone.

Figure: Dhamma Giri in Igatpuri

16.3 Dhamma Giri in Igatpuri

Apart from the Global Vipassana Pagoda in Mumbai and the various Vipassana retreats across India and abroad, there is also a site called Dhamma Giri, which is main centre of the Vipassana Research Institute in Igatpuri in Maharashtra, which has cells for individual meditators to do long term Vipassana meditation retreats.

Vipassana Research Institute runs a number of online courses in Pali and Buddhist meditation for those interested. One can see details on their website https://www.vridhamma.org/

16.4 Conclusion

In this chapter, we have discussed the Global Vipassana Pagoda in Mumbai, one of the main centers of SN Goenkaji's 10-day Vipassana retreat centers.

Chapter 17: Tibetan Monasteries in India

In this chapter, we discuss a few important Tibetan monasteries that are located in India. Most of them were set up by Tibetan refugee monks after they fled from Tibet after 1960s and came to India. Most of them have their parent monasteries in the Tibet region of China.

There are many Tibetan monasteries spread across India, and each Tibetan settlement such as Bylakuppe in Karnataka usually has branches of many of the other monasteries. However, in this chapter, we focus on only a few famous monasteries.

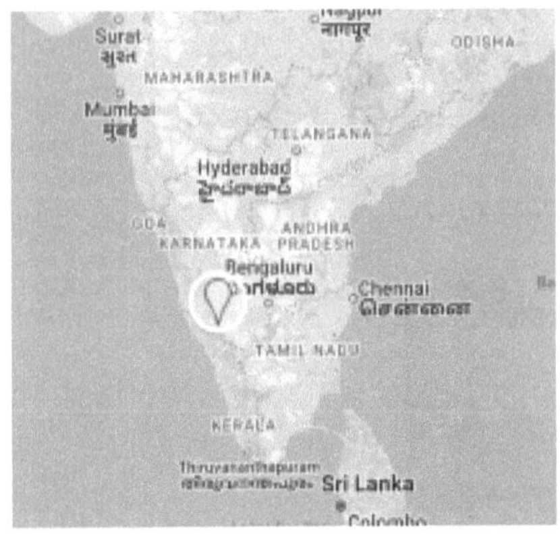

Figure: Location of Bylakuppe in South Karnataka state. Latitude: 12.4307° N, Longitude: 75.9718° E

17.1 How to get there

Bylakuppe, where many Tibetan refugee settlements and monasteries are located, is in South Karnataka state, about 2 hours drive from Mysore city. Mungdod, another Tibetan refugee settlement, is in

North Karnataka. One can hire a taxi or take a bus from Mysore to reach Bylakuppe.

Dharamsala, which is the seat of the Dalai lama, is another important site for Tibetan monasteries. So is Bir. Both are located in Himachal Pradesh state. Odisha and other states also have a few Tibetan monasteries.

Figure: Namdroling monastery in Bylakuppe

Figure: Tara temple in Namdroling monastery in Bylakuppe

Figure: Namdroling monastery

17.2 Namdroling monastery in Bylakuppe

Namdroling Monastery in India was founded by Penor Rinpoche, a very senior lama of the Nyingma tradition of Tibetan Buddhism. Its main temple in Tibet is called Palyul Monastery. It is one of the biggest monasteries in Bylakuppe. It holds Tibetan-style meditation retreats every year, in which both monks and lay people are welcome to participate. Thousands of monks study here for more than 10 years to become Khenpo and Lopen, who are qualified to teach Tibetan Buddhism

Figure: Sera Jey monastery in Bylakuppe

Figure: Commemoration pillar of Sera Jey monastery in Bylakuppe

17.3 Sera monastery in Bylakuppe

Sera Monastery is one of the great monasteries of the Gelugpa sect, to which His Holiness the Dalai Lama belongs. In India it includes the Sera Je and Sera Me monasteries. Thousands of monks study here. His Holiness the Dalai Lama also visits this monastery every year to give Buddhist teachings

Figure: Sakya monastery in Bylakuppe

Figure: Drikung Kagyu monastery in Bylakuppe

Figure: Tashi Lhunpo monastery in Bylakuppe

17.4 Other monasteries in Bylakuppe

Bylakuppe in South Karnataka is one of the biggest Tibetan refuggee settlements in India. It has a number of monasteries including Namdroling and Sera. Other monasteries in Bylakuppe include Sakya monastery, Tashi Lhunpo monastery and Drikung Kagyu monastery.

Figure: Gaden monastery building in Mungdod in Karnataka

17.5 Gaden monastery in Mungdod

Mungdod in North Karnataka is also a center for many monasteries. Gaden monastery is one of the huge Gelugpa monasteries in Mungdod. HH Dalai lama often visits to give teachings there.

Tibetan Buddhist Temple in McLeodganj, Dharamsala. By Adam Jones from Kelowna, BC, Canada - Main Street Temple - McLeod Ganj - Himachal Pradesh - India, CC BY-SA 2.0, https://commons.wikimedia.org/w/index.php?curid=64188759

17.6 Tsuglagkhang complex in McLeodganj, Dharamsala, Himachal Pradesh

McLeodGanj is the main seat of HH Dalai Lama and the Tibetan government in exile. It is a busy town with many Tibetan government organizations and temples, and a sizeable Tibetan refugee population. Tsuglagkhang complex in McLeodganj is the main temple of the Dalai Lama.

Figure: Sakya center monastery in Dehradun in Uttaranchal state

17.7 Sakya Center Buddhist monastery in Dehradun

The Sakya Centre Monastery in Dehradun (Uttarakhand) is the main seat of His Holiness Sakya Trizin, the head of the Sakya tradition. The monastery is set in beautiful expansive grounds and is well worth visiting.

17.8 Conclusion

In this chapter, we have discussed a few important Tibetan monasteries in India, including Namdroling, Sakya centre, Sera monastery, and Tsuglagkhang complex.

Chapter 18: Buddhist Places in Sikkim, Ladakh and Arunachal

In this chapter we discuss some of the important Buddhist sites in Sikkim, Ladakh (in Jammu and Kashmir) and Arunachal Pradesh. These areas are where Buddhists still form a substantial part of the population. Buddhists in these areas mainly follow Tibetan Buddhism.

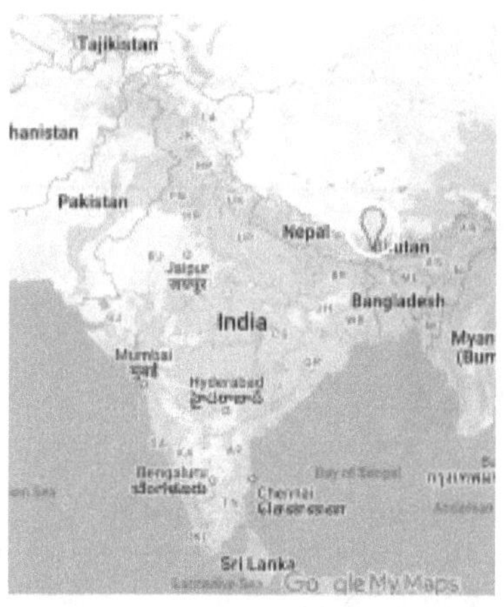

Figure: Location of Rumtek monastery in Sikkim state in North India. Latitude: 27.3331° N, Longitude: 88.6165° E

18.1 How to get there

Sikkim is a state close to north Bengal. The best way to reach Sikkim is by air to Bagdogra airport in north of West Bengal state, and take a taxi to Gangtok from there.

Leh can be reached by taking a flight to Leh airport, or alternatively taking a bus or taxi from Srinagar in Jammu and Kashmir.

The closest airport to Tawang monastery in Arunachal Pradesh state is Tezpur in Assam, one can take a taxi from there. Alternatively, one can fly to Guwahati airport in Assam and a take a taxi from there.

Figure: Rumtek monastery in Sikkim. By Vikramjit Kakati - Own work, CC BY-SA 3.0, https://commons.wikimedia.org/w/index.php?curid=19113031

Dubdi monastery in Sikkim. By Kothanda Srinivasan - Flickr, CC BY 2.0, https://commons.wikimedia.org/w/index.php?curid=9998112

Tashiding monastery in Sikkim. By walter callens - originally posted to Flickr as india - sikkim, CC BY 2.0, https://commons.wikimedia.org/w/index.php?curid=10317637

18.2 Buddhist sites in Sikkim state

Sikkim used to be an independent Buddhist kingdom prior to being absorbed as a state by India in 1975.

Important monasteries in Sikkim include the following:

- **Rumtek monastery**: It is the main seat of the Karmapa of the Karma Kagyu sect of Tibetan Buddhism. It is located 24 km from Gangtok, the capital of Sikkim state in India. It was established in 1740 AD. It is one of the most important Tibetan Buddhist monasteries in the world.
- **Dubdi monastery** (also called Yuksom monastery): It is one of the oldest and most significant monasteries in Sikkim, built in 1701 AD by Chogyar Namgyal.
- **Tashiding monastery**: it is an important monastery related to the Nyingma sect of Tibetan Buddhism. It was founded in 1641.
- **Pemayangtse monastery**: This is located 110 km west of the capital Gangtok. It was founded in 1647 and forms part of the Buddhist circuit of Sikkim. It belongs to the Nyingma sect.

- **Sanga Choeling monastery**: It was built in 1697 and is close to Pemayangtse monastery and also part of the Buddhist circuit.

Figure: Hemis monastery in Ladakh. By Bernard Gagnon Canon EOS REBEL T4i - Own work, CC BY-SA 4.0, https://commons.wikimedia.org/w/index.php?curid=76431590

Figure: Alchi monastery in Ladakh. By Steve Hicks - originally posted to Flickr as Alchi, CC BY 2.0, https://commons.wikimedia.org/w/index.php?curid=9033143

Figure: Thigse monastery in Ladakh. By Aksveer - Own work, CC BY-SA 4.0, https://commons.wikimedia.org/w/index.php?curid=76046385

18.3 Buddhist sites in Ladakh in Jammu and Kashmir

Ladakh (part of the Union Territory of Jammu & Kashmir) is home to magnificent Tibetan Buddhist monasteries perched on dramatic cliffs and hilltops. Important Buddhist sites in Ladakh include:

- **Hemis monastery**: This is the largest and a significant monastery in Ladakh. It is close to Leh, the capital of Ladakh. Famous for its annual Hemis Festival.
- **Shey monastery**: This is the former capital of Ladakh, ,with a large gilded copper Buddha.
- **Alchi monastery**: This is the oldest monastery of Ladakh, founded in 11th century AD. It has rare Kashmiri-influenced murals and sculptures.
- **Diksit Monastery**: This is located in Diksit, Nubra valley in Leh district of Ladakh. It is known for its giant Maitreya Buddha statue.
- **Thiksey monastery**: This has beautiful architecture. It is affiliated to the Gelugpa sect of Tibetan Buddhism. It is a remarkable 12-storey monastery with several temples.

Leh is best reached by flight from Delhi or Chandigarh, or by road from Srinagar.

Figure: Tawang monastery in Arunachal Pradesh

18.4 Buddhist sites in Arunachal Pradesh

Tawang Monastery is located in the remote Tawang district near the Bhutan and Tibet borders, Tawang is the largest Buddhist monastery in India and the second-largest in the world after Drepung in Tibet. It was founded in the 17th century and belongs to the Gelugpa tradition.

The nearest airport is Tezpur in Assam; taxi from there takes about 8 hours.

Figure: View of Rewalsar lake or Tso Pema lake with statue of Padmasambhava overlooking it

18.5 Buddhist sites in Himachal Pradesh

There are a few important Tibetan Buddhist sites in Himachal Pradesh at the foothills of the Himalayas. These include McLeodGanj (the seat of His Holiness Dalai Lama and Tibetan Government in Exile), Bir, Rewalsar and Lahaul and Spiti. A number of Tibetan monasteries, small and large, are scattered around these areas.

In particular, Rewalsar Lake (Tso Pema), in Himachal Pradesh, is one of the most sacred sites in Vajrayana Buddhism, associated with Guru Padmasambhava (Guru Rinpoche), the 8th-century tantric master who brought Buddhism to Tibet. Legends describe Guru Padmasambhava meditating here and a cave with his footprints is located nearby. A large statue of Guru Padmasambhava overlooks the lake, which is circumambulated by pilgrims of both the Buddhist and Hindu and Sikh traditions. Several Tibetan, Nyingma and other monasteries surround the lake.

There is also a cave with the footprints of Guru Padmasambhava, a few kilometers from Rewalsar Lake.

18.6 Conclusion

In this chapter, we have discussed a few important Buddhist monasteries in Sikkim, Ladakh and Arunachal Pradesh.

Chapter 19: Buddhism Related Sections of Indian Museums

In this chapter we discuss some of the Buddhist artifacts on display in various big museums in India in the metro cities of New Delhi, Mumbai, Chennai and Kolkata.

This is in addition to several on-site museums such as the ones in Amarawati, Nagarjunakonda, Nalanda etc.

Figure: Gateway of the Bharhut stupa, at the Indian museum in Kolkata

Figure: Casket containing Buddha's relics, at the Indian museum in Kolkata

19.1 Buddhist displays at the Indian Museum in Kolkata

Indian museum in Kolkata is one of the premier museums in India.

Some of the interesting Buddhism related artifacts in the Indian museum are as follows:

- **Bharhut** is a stupa ruins site located in Madhya pradesh. In the Indian museum Kolkata they have a magnificient exhibition where the entire gate and railings (carved on wood or stone magnificiently) have been assembled inside the museum. It was quite a site to see.
- The second Buddhist exhibit was part of the Bodh Gaya temple's pillars. It said that the Bodh Gaya pillars had a 3D carvings that were even superior to the Bharhut stupa exhibit.
- The next exhibits are several stone and terracota images of the Buddha and Bodhisattvas, lots of very minute carvings from the buddha's life. A few of the statues were on loan to an international exhibition in China.
- The next was an exhibition of gold and silver coins from

Kanishka's, Mauryan and other ages.

- Another section had a mud model of stupa and actual Buddha relics were displayed.
- Finally there is an exhibit from Rangoon, Burma where the entire temple model (along with precious gems) has been dismantled and reassembled in the museum. The construction of the temple is done very elegantly.
- Another exhibit has a burmese style buddha statue. These were brought to Kolkata after the british conquest of burma in the 19th century.

The museum entry was Rs 10 for Indians and Rs 50 extra for the permission to take photos. The prices are subject to change.

Figure: Casket containing Buddhist relics, at the national museum in New Delhi

Figure: Buddhist pilgrims worshipping at the relics hall, at the national museum in New Delhi

Figure: An ivory tusk carved with scenes from Buddha's life, at the National museum in New Delhi

19.2 Buddhist displays at National Museum in New Delhi

The national museum in New Delhi has a huge and comprehensive buddhist collection, including the following:

- Buddhist relics kept in a casket donated by Thai government
- Paintings display from Chinese Donhuang caves on silk road
- An embedded life of buddha in ivory, going in s spiral fashion, in the ivory section
- A huge section of buddhist images in bronze Buddha images in wood and stone, from different times and origins
- Ajanta paintings (in Ajanta section)
- Buddha States from Mauryan, Kushana dynasties (in Maurya, Kushana sections)
- Bronzes of avalokiteshwara etc (in Bronzes section)

Entry fees for indian nationals is Rs 50 for the museum, higher for foreigners, all prices are subject to change.

Recently, the Buddhist section has been housed in a separate building complex just outside the main museum building. It includes the relics as well. It has seven galleries including the following:

- Thangka Paintings
- The Buddha's relics in a casket
- Jataka stories
- Indian impressions of Buddha
- Chinese and Tibetan and other Asian Buddhas

Figure: Tibetan Buddhism section at the Prince of Wales museum in Mumbai

Figure: Art of Gandhara section at the Prince of Wales museum in Mumbai

19.3 Buddhist displays at the Prince of Wales museum in Mumbai (now called Chattrapati Shivaji Maharaj Vastu Sanghrahalaya)

CSM, formerly called Prince of Wales museum is the finest museum in Mumbai, possibly in India.

Buddhist related exhibits in the are as follows:

- A good sculpture section with scenes from the Buddha's life.
- A section on a Gandharan stupa recently excavated in Pakistan.
- A rich Tibetan section with thangkas, statues and interactive displays.
- Chinese and Japanese pottery.
- A Gandhara Art section displaying the Greco-Buddhist sculptural tradition.

Entry to the museum in 2022 costs Rs 75 plus 50 for camera. However, prices are subject to change.

Figure: Parts of Amarawati stupa, in Chennai government museum

Figure: Section of Amarawati stupa on display at government museum in Chennai

19.4 Buddhist displays at the government museum in Chennai

The Government Museum in Chennai houses the most important collection of Amaravati stupa panels in India, large carved limestone slabs depicting scenes from the Buddha's life and Jataka tales in the distinctive Amaravati style. The collection rivals the Amaravati Room at the British Museum. Also displayed are bronzes and stone Buddha and Bodhisattva figures from various South Indian periods.

19.5 Conclusion

In this chapter, we have discussed various Buddhist artifacts displayed in museums across India.

Chapter 20: Buddhist places in Sri Lanka: Cultural triangle

In this chapter, we review a few Buddhist places in Sri Lanka. Sri Lanka is an ancient Buddhist country which has Buddhism for thousands of years. Buddhism was brought here from India by emperor Ashoka's son Mahinda, who planted the sapling from the original Bodhi at Anuradhapura.

Buddhist places in Sri Lanka include the cultural triangle consisting of Anuradhapura, Dambulla, and Polonnaruwa. Kandy, the city of the temple of the tooth, is also an important Buddhist holy city.

Figure: Kandy in central Sri Lanka, site of Sri Dalada Maligawa temple of the tooth. Latitude: 7.2936° N, Longitude: 80.6414° E

Location & Access

Colombo Bandaranaike International Airport is the main entry point.

Accessible by taxi or bus from the airport to Kandy, Anuradhapura and other cities.

Best time to visit: December to April (dry season in most of the island).

20.1 How to get there

Colombo airport is the main airport in Sri Lanka and is accessible from many major airlines.

From Colombo airport one can either take taxi or bus. There is a direct bus to Kandy from Kerunegela bus stand, which is a very short distance from Colombo airport.

Or else, one can travel from Colombo airport to the main bus stand in Colombo city and take buses to Kandy or Anuradhapura etc from there.

Figure: Entrance to Sri Dalada Maligawa Buddha tooth temple in Kandy

Figure: Inside temple of the tooth Sri Dalada Maligawa in Kandy

Figure: Moat around the temple of the tooth in Kandy

Figure: Decorated moonstone at the temple of the tooth in Kandy

20.2 Sri Dalada Maligawa Buddha tooth temple in Kandy

Sri Dalada Maligawa is the most sacred temple in Sri Lanka, as it houses the Buddha tooth relic. It is a very lively place and one can sit in peace and watch the multitude of humanity here offering flowers and performing other ceremonies. Once or twice a day, a relic of the Buddha is taken out, displayed and worshipped. There is also a big festival once a year when the relic is taken in a procession. There are a few museums in the vicinity, including the International Buddhist Museum, that are worth visiting.

The tooth relic of Buddha is located in the Relic Room on the first floor. Many worshipers can be seen sitting or meditating reverently in the temple, offering beautiful lotus flowers and other offerings.

The whole complex has wonderful architecture. It also has a Dalada Museum and a wonderful International Buddhist Museum.

A hall has gifts from Thai and Burmese and Buddha's feet etc., and an exhibition of the history of Dalada Temple. The tooth relic of the Buddha was originally brought to Sri Lanka from India by two ministers fleeing from war. It was said that it brought rain where there was drought. There is a legend that the one who owned Dalada ruled Sri Lanka. The relic of the tooth passed through various capitals including Anuradhapura and Polonnaruwa before reaching the Kandyan kingdom and finally the British.

Outside the Dalada Maligawa Temple, visitors have to deposit all bags and also deposit their shoes. For foreigners, the ticket entry fee in 2019 was 1000 LKR and for SAARC nationals it was 500 LKR, although prices are subject to change. There is a thorough security check before entering the premises, as this place has once been the target of a terrorist attack.

Figure: International Buddhist museum building in Kandy, located close to Sri Dalada Maligawa truth temple complex

20.3 International Buddhist museum in Kandy

The International Buddhist Museum is located right next to the Dalada Maligawa temple complex. The entry fee for foreign nationals is LKR

500, subject to change. It has a large Sri Lankan Buddhism section, with scale models of various monastic complexes and an overview of the history of both Theravada and Mahayana Buddhism in Sri Lanka. There were also statues of Avalokiteshvara in Sri Lanka, which suggests that Mahayana Buddhism was present there at one time, although only Theravada Buddhism is dominant today. The museum has information about the historical rivalry between the Abhayagiri vs Jetavana monasteries. Abhayagiri was open to Mahayana doctrines from India, while Jetavana stuck to Theravada. There was a part of the Buddha's tooth relic and a casket used to hold the relic. It has a section with information about the annual temple festival, with processions on elephants.

The museum also has sections from different Buddhist countries.

- There is a Bangadeshi section with ruins of several ancient monasteries found in Bangladesh.
- The Burmese section contains information about the life of a Burmese child undergoing initiation to become a monk as a ritual. There is also an overview of the Shwedagon Pagoda, which is built like a mandala. Each layer of that mandala represents a different concept such as suffering, the Buddha, the world of men, etc. It also has an overview of pagodas in Bagan Adi and the new capital, and a display of a complete Burmese temple with all its components.
- The Thai section has a display of the King of Thailand who is like the Dharma King or Bodhisattva, protector of the Dharma. It also has an overview of various ancient monasteries like Bangkok and the Lanna Kingdom, Sukhothai etc.
- The upper floor of the museum houses a Malaysian Buddhism section, which explains how since the ancient kingdoms of Sri Vijay, Malaysian monks and laymen have been re-emerging

and spreading Buddhism. It has exhibitions related to the Sri Lankan temple in Malaysia and the Chinese style temple in the Malaysian island of Penang. It also featured a Malaysian Buddhist temple, each floor in a different style, the base Chinese octagonal, the middle Thai and the top Burmese pagoda.

- The Indonesian section tells about the Buddhist history of Indonesia and has a scale model of the wonderful mandala-like temple at Borobodur

- The Indonesian section spoke of its history and the amazing temple like a mandala at borobodur, had a scale model too.

- The Vietnam section has exhibitions related to the important Buddhist temples of Hue and Hanoi and Saigon.

- An interesting part in the China section is how a tooth relic of Buddha was excavated from an underground temple after thousands of years. It contains a section of the four sacred Buddhist hills of China, such as Manjushri Wutai Mountain and others. It also describes Theravada Buddhism in China and Theravada temples in Yunnan 164 Province in China. It describes friendship with the Chinese Buddhist Association and Sri Lanka. It describes the different types and sects of Chinese Buddhism.

- The Japan section describes how all the various Buddhist schools flourished in their most developed form in Japan. It displays a Japanese monk's bowl, robes, colored paper lanterns and decorations, paintings, etc. It talks separately about all the traditions of Dōgen Zen, the esoteric traditions, the Pure Land school, Nichiren, etc.

- The Korean section houses a Korean temple and the monk's bowl and temple bell, etc.

- There is an extensive Indian Buddhism section, which details the various Buddhist monasteries and temples located in

India.

Figure: Sri Maha Bodhi tree in Anuradhapura

20.4 Sri Maha Bodhi tree in Anuradhapura

Sri Maha Bodhi is one of the holiest places in Sri Lanka, after the tooth temple. It is built out of a sapling of the main Bodhi tree in Bodhgaya where the Buddha meditated and became enlightened. Later the original tree was destroyed in India but was re-planted with a sapling of this Sri Lankan Mahabodhi tree.

The Mahabodhi tree in Anuradhapura has been continuously guarded by soldiers, priests etc. for more than 2000 years. Many revered worshipers are found chanting suttas and praying near the tree. There are also a lot of monkeys in the area.

Figure: Ruwanveli maha stupa in Anuradhapura, along with elephant statues

Figure: Signboard showing location of different stupas in Anuradhapura

Figure: Lankarama stupa in Anuradhapura

Figure: Ancient Abhayagiri stupa in Anuradhapura

Figure: Twin pond in Anuradhapura, where the monks went to take a bath

Figure: Jetavana vihara in Anuradhapura

20.5 Monasteries in Anuradhapura

Anuradhapura is the ancient capital of Sri Lanka and peak of the cultural triangle. There are a number of important monasteries there including the following:

- **Abhayagiri monastery**: Abhayagiri is a huge ancient monastic complex. There is a huge circular pond, beside it there are beautiful moon rocks, there is a historical exhibition in it. Many Sri Lankan devotees walk around the huge monastery dressed in white. Its stupa rivalled the Ruwanwelisaya in size.
- **Lankaramaya**: This has the design of a nice neat monastery complex with the following components: Lake outside, living quarters (several), administrative quarters, the main stupa, Bodhi tree shrine.
- **Vessagiri cave complex**: This is a cave complex where monks used to meditate under stones and huge rock boulders. They had cut seats, stairs, even water lines into the rocks. There are

also some paintings on some rocks which are now damaged. There are some inscriptions in 169 Old Sinhalese language on other rocks. It also has a vantage point from where the three great pagodas, Sigiriya and other sights can be seen.

- **Thuparamaya dagoba**: The oldest stupa in Sri Lanka, enshrining the collarbone relic of the Buddha. It is a complete complex, small but also very beautiful. Some parts are still in ruins. Crowds of worshipers can be seen offering flowers and circumambulating the stupa, and monks can be seen chanting suttas.

- **Ruwanvesaliya**: The Ruwanveli stupa and monastery complex is huge in size. It is an ancient stupa, built by King Duthugamunu in the 4th century AD. It is a huge and vibrant stupa in size. It is still a very popular place and object of worship, painted white and has a lot of visitors and worshippers. Many devotees circumambulate the huge stupa. There are images of elephants all around. There are also statues of the king and queen who built the stupa. It is really peaceful, although crowded.

- **Jetavana Vihara**: This is one of the oldest Viharas and is very important historically. It belonged to the orthodox sect Theravada in rivalry with Abhaya Giri (Mahayana). It is a colossal structure comparable in size to the Pyramids of Giza in Egypt, and can be called one of the wonders of the ancient world. There is also a huge banyan tree outside.

Figure: Exterior of the cave temple in Dambulla, Sri Lanka

Figure: Sitting and standing Buddha statues in Dambulla cave temple in Sri Lanka

Figure: Stupa with sitting Buddhas in Dambulla cave temple in Sri Lanka

Figure: Painting on the wall of Dambulla cave temple in Sri Lanka

Figure: Statue of the Kandy king along with sitting Buddhas in Dambulla cave temple

20.6 Dambulla cave temples

The Dambulla Cave Temples are amazing rock-cut caves filled with Buddha images. In some caves, low lighting has been arranged to preserve the paintings. They are probably influenced by the paintings of the Ajanta caves in India and are in the same style. There are five caves in total. The entrance from the Golden Temple side is at the top of the hill after climbing more than 350 steps. Be careful buying tickets before starting the climb, as the ticket office at the top may be closed. Separate the Kings' entrance steps from the car park. The entry ticket for foreigners costs 1500 LKR in 2021, but prices are subject to change.

The Dambulla cave temple is on top of a rocky hillock, and can be viewed only after climbing many steps. There are many monkeys during the climb. At the temple itself, the monkeys were kept away via electric wire. The cave temple is quite unique. There are white decorative entrances built in Portuguese church style, before entering the actual caves.

Characteristics of some of the cave temples are as follows:

- The first cave temple has buddhas carved out of solid rock.
- The second temple is the best of the lot, with the sitting buddhas around the stupa. It is quite huge.
- The last three were built later, and are a bit less sophisticated. One of the temples has the tamil indian king of kandy's image as well, since it was him, one of the last kings of kandy, who renovated that cave temple.

Figure: Vatadage in Polonnaruwa

Figure: Standing Buddha statue in Lankatilaka vihara in Polonnaruwa

Figure: Sitting Buddha statue in Gal Vihara in Polonnaruwa

Figure: Standing and sleeping Buddha in Gal Vihara in Polonnaruwa

20.7 Temples in Polonnaruwa

Polonnaruwa is one of the ancient capitals of Sri Lanka. The archeological zone in Polonnaruwa has a numbe rof amazing temples including the following temples:

- **Vatadage**: The vadatage is simply magnificent in its beauty and symmetry. It is within the sacred quadrangle at Polonnaruwa. It is a circular stupa, largely intact and very well maintained. The moonstone is amazing. It has several buddha statues of sitting buddha. It is one of the highlights of polonnaruwa.
- **Kiri Vihara**: Kiri Vihara is the only completely intact stupa within the Polonnaruwa ruins. It is in the middle of a huge monastic complex with living quarters, library, meditation room, kitchen etc of the monks.
- **Lankatilaka Vihara**: Lankatilaka is within a complex of ancient temples. It has a huge standing buddha in the centre, and lots of carvings on the walls.
- **Gal Vihara**: It is one of the most visited and famous places in

polonnaruwa. Has 4 buddhas in different postures: 2 sitting buddhas in meditative posture, one standing buddha and one in sleeping posture. Also has ancient sinhala inscriptions on a rock face by king Parakramabahu. The whole thing was cut from solid rock, reflecting the skill of the craftsmen.

Figure: View of the lion rock at Sigiriya

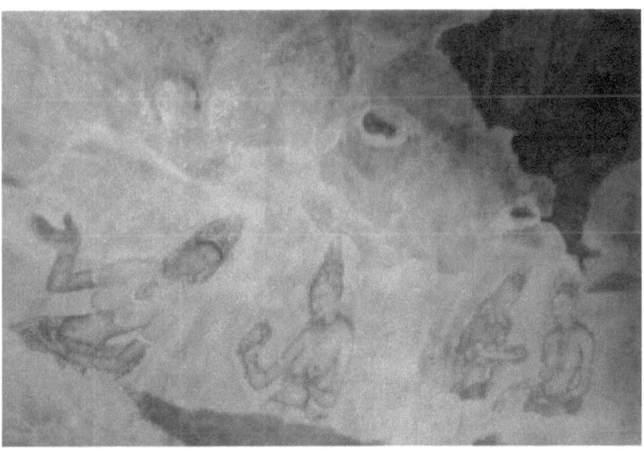

Figure: Paintings on the lion rock at Sigiriya

Figure: Climbing the lion rock at Sigiriya

20.8 Sigiriya lion rock

The Sigiriya Rock Palace is a palace built by King Kassapa in the 5th century on top of a hill in fear of his relative and rival. However, the rival later invaded with an army and conquered it. It is a palace built on top of a solid rock. There are several Buddhist cave temples on some parts of the rock. Perhaps there is a long history of rock behind this. It takes a traveler at least 3 hours to climb the stairs and reach the top and then come back down.

20.9 Conclusion

In this chapter, we have discussed a few important Buddhist palces in Sri Lanka.

Chapter 21: Buddhist places near Kathmandu in Nepal: Swayambhunath, Boudhanath and Patan

In this chapter, we discuss some of the principal sites that are related to Buddhism in Nepal. Lumbini, the birthplace of the Buddha, we have already discussed in chapter 4 earlier in this book.

Near Kathmandu, there are quite a few amazing ancient Buddhist temple sand stupas. Chief among them are Boudhanath stupa, as well as Swayambhunath stupa. There are also a few beautiful Newari Buddhist temples in Patan including Hiranyavarna Mahavihar and Rudravarna Mahavihar. There is also the Namo Buddha temple a few hours drive away from Kathmandu.

Figure: Location of Boudhanath stupa in Kathmandu in Nepal. Latitude: 27.7215° N, Longitude: 85.3616° E

Location & Access

Tribhuvan International Airport, Kathmandu, is the main entry point.

Taxis available from airport to all main sites in the valley.

Best time to visit: October–November or March–April.

21.1 How to get there

Kathmandu airport is the main airport in Nepal. From the airport one can take a taxi to the various Buddhist places including Boudhanath, Swayambhunath and Patan.

Figure: Boudhanath stupa in Kathmandu, Nepal

Figure: Map of monasteries around Boudhanath in Kathmandu, Nepal

Figure: Devotees circumambulating Boudhanath stupa

21.2 Boudhanath stupa in Kathmandu

Boudhanath is a UNESCO world heritage site located close to Kathmandu Airport and Pashupatinath. It is the biggest and holiest buddhist stupa in the world.

Throughout the day, thousands of pilgrims circumambulate the stupa in a clockwise direction, while chanting mantras or making prostrations. There are many shops selling thangka paintings and puja objects such as mala, and more than ten buddhist temples and monasteries all around the stupa. The place usually gets more crowded in the evening.

There is a ticket for foreigners, costing around 500 Nepali Rupees in 2019, but the amount could have increased since.

Figure: Swayambhunath stupa in Kathmandu, Nepal

Figure: Smaller stupas next to Swayambhunath Stupa

21.3 Swayambhunath stupa in Kathmandu

Swayambhunath, often called the 'Monkey Temple', perches atop a wooded hill overlooking the Kathmandu Valley. It is one of the oldest and most important Buddhist monuments in Nepal, revered by both Buddhists and Hindus. Its great gilded stupa is ringed by smaller shrines, vajras, prayer wheels and statues. The climb involves over 300 steps. Harmless monkeys are everywhere. From the summit, the views over Kathmandu are magnificent. The all-seeing eyes of the Buddha painted on all four sides of the stupa's harmika are the iconic symbol of Nepal.

Entry: Nepali Rupees 100 for Indians, higher for others. It is an absolute must-see for any visitor to Nepal.

One can do Kora circumambulations around the stupa, in clockwise direction. It is located at a few kilometers distance from Thamel in Kathmandu.

Figure: Shrine in Hiranyagarbha Mahavihar in Patan

Figure: Shrines in Hiranyagarbha Mahavihar in Patan

Figure: Hiranyavarna Mahavihar in Patan

21.4 Hiranyavarna Mahavihar in Patan, also called Kwa Bahal or Golden Temple

This is a beautiful Newari Buddhist temple. The architecture is traditional Nepali, with an outer and inner courtyard. It is located at a close walking distance from Patan Darbar Square. There are lots of sculptures inside the temple. The main shrine is of Shakyamuni Buddha.

Some ancient Sanskrit Vajrayana Buddhist texts are kept here, the Bajracharya teachers can explain and recite the texts and perform pujas. There is an entry fee.

Figure: Entrance to Rudravarna Mahavihar in Patan, Nepal

Figure: Rudravarna Mahavihar main shrine

21.5 Okul Bahal or Rudra Varna Mahavihar in Patan

It is a very nice and peaceful Buddhist temple in elegant traditional Newari style. Combined Entrance fee is Rupees 50 for foreigners (subject to change), which gives entry to Mahaboudha temple also.

Figure: Mahabuddha temple in Patan. It was undergoing renovation when visited by the author.

21.6 Mahabuddha temple in Patan

This temple is located just next to the Rudravarna mahavihar. This is a beautiful Buddhist temple built in a model resembling the Bodhgaya Mahabodhi temple in India. The entry fee is Rupees 50 valid for two temples. Damaged in the 2015 earthquake but now restored.

Figure: Patan museum building

21.7 Patan Museum

The Patan Museum occupies the Royal Palace in Patan Durbar Square and has an outstanding section on Vajrayana Buddhist art, including bronzes, ritual objects, and explanatory panels that greatly illuminate the complex iconography of Newar and Tibetan Buddhism. It is considered one of the best museum displays of Buddhist art in South Asia.

21.8 Four Ashoka Stupas in Four Directions in Patan

According to tradition, Emperor Ashoka himself visited Patan (then called Lalitpur) during his great pilgrimage and built four stupas marking the four cardinal directions. These four modest but historically significant stupas: Lagan Thura (South), Teta Thura (East), Pucho Thura (West) and Ibahi Thura (North), survive today as distinctive landmarks in the old city.

21.9 Namo Buddha

Namo Buddha is a sacred site about 40 km southeast of Kathmandu, associated with a past life of the Buddha. According to tradition, the Bodhisattva in a former life offered his body to a starving tigress and her cubs. A stupa marks the site. The surrounding hilltop monastery and the journey through beautiful Nepalese countryside make this a rewarding half-day excursion from Kathmandu.

21.10 Conclusion

In this chapter, we have discussed a few important Buddhist places to visit around Kathmandu valley in Nepal.

Chapter 22: Buddhist places in Bhutan: Tiger's Nest in Paro

In this chapter we discuss some of the important Buddhist places in Bhutan.

Figure: Location of Paro Taktsang Tiger's nest monastery in Paro in Bhutan. Latitude: 27.4918° N, Longitude: 89.3634° E

Location & Access

Paro International Airport is the only international airport in Bhutan.

Druk Air and Bhutan Airlines operate flights from Kolkata, Delhi, Bangkok and other cities.

All tourists (except Indian, Bangladeshi and Maldivian nationals) must arrange visits through a licensed Bhutanese tour operator.

Nearest Indian airport: Bagdogra (North Bengal).

22.1 How to get there

Bhutan has an airport in Paro. One can take a flight to Paro airport. Alternatively, the closest Indian airport to Bhutan is Bagdogra airport in North Bengal, and for some travelers it might be easier and cheaper to take a flight to Bagdogra airport and get a taxi to Bhutan from there.

Figure: Tiger's nest Paro Taktsang temple in Paro, Bhutan

Figure: Meditation cave in Bhutan near Tiger's Nest temple, wheer Yeshe Tsogyal, the enlightened consort of Guru Rinpoche meditated

Figure: Tiger's nest temple in Paro

22.2 Paro Taktsang or Tiger's nest in Paro, Bhutan

Paro Taktsang (Tiger's Nest Monastery) is the most sacred site in Bhutan and one of the most visually dramatic in all of Asia. It clings to a sheer granite cliff 900 metres above the Paro Valley floor, seemingly defying gravity. According to Vajrayana tradition, Guru Padmasambhava (Guru Rinpoche), the 8th-century master who brought Buddhism to Tibet, flew here on the back of a transformed tigress (actually his consort Yeshe Tsogyal in transformed form) and meditated in a cave for three months.

The monastery, built around this cave in 1692, is one of about 13 Taktsang ('Tiger's Nest') sites across the Himalayan world. The climb to the monastery takes 2–3 hours on foot, with a halfway cafeteria for a rest stop. Walking sticks are available for hire at the base. The path passes mantras carved on rocks, small stupas and stone cairns. Mobile phones and cameras must be deposited at the entrance; a traditional Bhutanese dress (kira or gho) is required inside and is available to borrow. Inside the complex, multiple temple rooms surround the main meditation cave of Guru Padmasambhava. One may meditate in the cave and seek the blessings of the sacred site. The views of the Paro Valley below are spectacular.

Paro Taktsang is the most sacred place in Bhutan, one of about 18 tiger nests. They are called so because Padmasambhava Guru Rinpoche flew there on the back of a tiger and meditated there. It is built on a rock and one has to climb 3000 feet to see it. It is at the end of an arduous journey for those who find hiking difficult. It is incredibly beautiful and the most sacred place in Bhutan. It is wonderful to meditate in Padmasambhava's cave, there is peaceful energy everywhere in that cave.

Author's personal experience:

It was a long journey till Paro Taktsang. We were staying at a Buddhist monk's home in a village near Paro, where his kind mother took care of us and gave us food and a warm bed to sleep in. We had booked a taxi the previous day, and took the taxi in the morning, although the driver was late by an hour. We passed by Paro airport and a palace called "Dzong" on the way. Finally, around 8 am, our 191 car reached the bottom of the hill we had to climb to reach Paro Taktsang Monastery.

We bought some walking sticks for Rs.50. Then we started our journey upstairs. The weather was a bit difficult to breathe, the air was cold, the water was icy and I was freezing. I had two Bhutanese friends with me, they were very kind and didn't allow me to take anything, they took food and everything.

First, we came over a stream where one could drink water from three rivers, we drank some fresh but icy cold water. My hands almost froze. There were two or more ways to go up. The main road was well maintained, had seats and water along the way. But my friends insisted on adopting a shortcut which is shorter but faster. The steep climb left me out of breath and my slippers kept slipping. My kind friends kept helping me climb.

Eventually we reached the halfway point, a cafe, stopped for a few minutes to catch our breath and started again within half an hour (instead of the hour or more that it usually takes on the long route). We passed mantras carved on rocks, small stupas, stones stacked one on top of the other. It had a magical feel to it, although I was probably so tired and out of breath that I didn't really notice. Some dogs acted as our guardians and gently encouraged me to complete the climb.

After about two hours of walking we reached the main gate of Paro Taktsang. On the way we saw many small caves built as the abode of great yogis. We passed by a place where the sign of the achievement of a Siddha Guru was a never-ending supply of water gushing out of a rock. We drank water and felt very light and refreshed. We kept climbing and climbing for over an hour until we came to the equivalent of the monastery but on a different rock, then went down a steep set of stairs with railings. Various colorful thangkas were lit all along the way. The views of the Paro Valley 192 were also stunning. Then there was Yeshe Tsogyal's cave with steep steps. But we did not enter it on the way, but saw it on the way back.

When we entered the Taktsang Monastery, we deposited all the documents and mobile phones etc at the reception and entered the monastery with my wallet and clothes, I wore a traditional Bhutanese dress which was given to me by a kind friend. We could only stay half an hour in the main cave where Guru Rinpoche meditated, as it was too early for tourists to arrive.

The complex had many chambers and secret places. In one room the monks were doing some protective prayers so we were not allowed inside. There was a custom of giving a small offering and then throwing three dice and depending on the number your wish could come true.

There was a stone containing the sacred terma. The second stone had the Eye of Knowledge, you close your eyes and walk towards the stone with outstretched hand, if you touch that stone your wish can come true. In another room was a statue of Avalokiteshvara, in the next room was a statue of Maitreya, in another room was a statue of Guru Rinpoche. An underground chamber covered the actual cave where Guru Padmasambhava meditated. If you meditate in a room, your wish should come true. In one room was a book about the Namdroling empowerment of Penor Rinpoche's body. Another chamber contained a stupa, which was rebuilt after the fire with the help of funds raised from the Japanese and the Bhutanese government. It also had a dot which allegedly represented the head of Vajrayogini.

The place was holy, full of magic. The famous Buddhist teacher Chogyam Trungpa Rinpoche also spent a lot of time meditating here at Takhtsang, where he wrote a sacred text called The Practice of Mahamudra.

We spent about an hour in total at the Paro Taktsang temple complex. Looking down, the views of the Paro Valley were amazing as expected. Perhaps realized Buddhist masters are still meditating in the vast forests. Eventually, we had to come back around 11:30 or 12 in the morning. We also had lunch on the way. The way down was much easier than going up. At the base was a forest of deodar trees. People were selling all kinds of souvenirs.

Figure: Kyichu Lakhang temple in Paro

22.3 Kyichu Lakhang, the oldest temple in Paro

Kyichu Lakhang is the oldest temple in Paro. It is a stone temple. the courtyard had an orange tree that produced oranges all year, miraculously. It also has an adjoining cremation ground. The complex was surrounded by beautiful Bhutanese paddy fields. It is said to have been built in the 7th century CE by the Tibetan emperor Songtsen Gampo, even before the arrival of Padmasambhava in Bhutan.

The main shrine has multiple statues of Avalokiteshwara, the ten headed and thousand hand one, as well as of Sakyamuni buddha. It also had a seat of a senior Kagyu lama. The adjoining temple was where Dilgo Khyentse Rinpoche's relics were kept, who was one of the most revered Nyingma masters of the 20th century. It also has a statue of Padmasambhava.

Figure: Karbandi monastery in Phuentsholing

22.4 Karbandi monastery in Phuentsholing

The Karbandi Monastery, perched on a hill above the border town of Phuentsholing, is a beautiful Kagyu monastery with white stupas and a large Guru Rinpoche statue.

It seems lots of Indian couples from Bengal visit this monastery, there is a rumor that couples who wish so might be blessed with a child after visiting this monastery. The monastery is on a high point overlooking the Bengal town of Jaigaon. It is quite beautiful and picturesque and has lots of white beautiful stupas. There is a huge statue of Guru Rinpoche, Shakyamuni surrounded by Shariputra and Maudgalanya and Lama Shedrup who founded Bhutan by uniting the warring tribes. There were beautiful paintings from the Jataka tales, the 4 guardians and so on.

The residence of the Je Khenpo (the religious head of Bhutan) is located nearby. The walls are decorated with Jataka tale paintings and traditional iconography.

Figure: Buddha Dordenma statue in Thimpu

22.5 Buddha Dordenma statue in Thimpu

The Buddha Dordenma is a colossal gilded bronze Buddha statue (51.5 metres tall) enthroned on a hilltop overlooking Thimpu, Bhutan's capital. Built to fulfil a prophecy and funded largely by Singaporean devotees, it houses 125,000 smaller Buddha images and a large meditation hall within its base. The statue is still in its finishing stages of development.

It is also meant to be a meditation complex, the big hall under the buddha statue. My friend told me the eye is made of diamond and costs like 25 crore Ngultrim.

22.6 Conclusion

In this chapter, we have discussed a few important Buddhist sites in Bhutan, including Paro Taktsang or Tiger's nest monastery.

Chapter 23: Buddhist places in Bangladesh: Paharpur and Jagaddala Mahavihara

In this chapter, we discuss important Buddhist sites in Bangladesh, namely Somapura mahavihar (also called Paharpur Buddhist monastery) and Jagaddala mahavihar and a modern living monastery in Dhaka.

Figure: Location of Somapura (Paharpur) mahavihara in Bangladesh. Latitude: 25.0276° N, Longitude: 88.9750° E

23.1 How to get there

The main airport in Bangladesh is Dhaka. It is best to take a flight to Dhaka and from there to hire a taxi to visit the monasteries. Somapura or Paharpur is located in the Rajshahi district in west of Bangaldesh.

Figure: Paharpur Buddhist monastery. By Abdulmominbd - Own work, CC BY-SA 4.0, https://commons.wikimedia.org/w/ index.php?curid=82707878

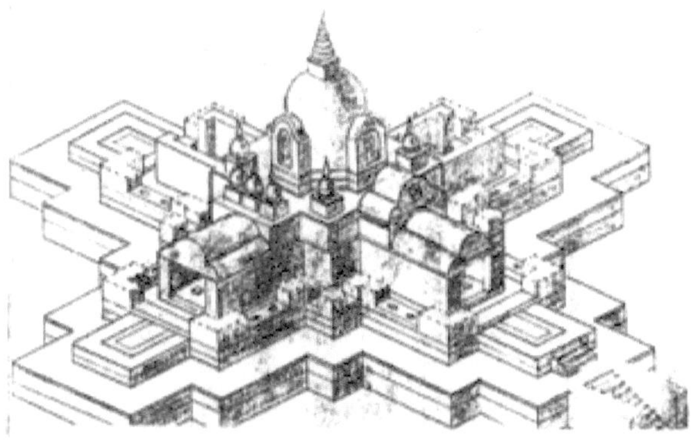

Figure: Model of Paharpur Buddhist monastery. By hafizur rahaman - bdheritage.info, CC BY 3.0, https://commons.wikimedia.org/w/ index.php?curid=13665586

23.2 Somapura Mahavihar (Paharpur Buddhist monastery)

Somapura Mahavihara, also known as Paharpur, is a UNESCO World Heritage Site in the Rajshahi district of northwestern Bangladesh. It is one of the greatest Buddhist monasteries of the ancient world, covering 27 acres. Built by the Pala king Dharmapala in the 8th century CE, it accommodated approximately 1,000 monks at its peak. The monastery's distinctive stepped-pyramid plan directly influenced Buddhist architecture in Burma, Java (Indonesia) and other parts of Southeast Asia. The site is best reached from Dhaka by flying or bus to Rajshahi and then hiring a taxi to Paharpur.

Figures: Ruins of Jagaddala Mahavihar. By Toruxsoftware - Own work, CC   BY-SA   4.0,   https://commons.wikimedia.org/w/ index.php?curid=52140713

23.3 Jagaddala Mahavihar

Jagaddala Mahavihara was built in the 11th century CE by the later Pala kings in the Varendra region of northern Bangladesh. It was one of the last great Buddhist universities of the ancient world before the Pala dynasty was displaced and Buddhism declined in Bengal. Only ruins now remain.

Figure: Gate of the Dharmarajika Buddhist monastery in Dhaka. By Ifteebd10 - Own work, CC BY-SA 4.0, https://commons.wikimedia.org/w/index.php?curid=126853919

23.4 Dharmarajika Buddhist monastery in Dhaka

The Dharmarajika Buddhist Monastery in the capital city of Dhaka is the main living Theravada monastery complex in Bangladesh, serving as the head monastery for Bangladeshi Buddhism. It is a working monastery open to respectful visitors.

23.5 Conclusion

In this chapter, we have discussed ancient monasteries in Bangladesh, namely Paharpur and Jagaddala Mahavihar, as well as a modern living monastery in Dhaka.

Chapter 24: Buddhist places in Pakistan: Taxila and Peshawar

In this chapter, we discuss Taxila, an important Buddhist place of learning located in Pakistan. We also discuss Shaji ki Dheri in Peshawar, site of an important Gandhara era Buddhist monastery. Another important Buddhist holy place in Pakistan is Oddiyana, where Guru Rinpoche Padmasambhava was born.

Northern Pakistan was the site of the ancient Greco Bactrian kingdom of Gandhara, which had a huge influence on buddha statues and buddhist art. The empire of Kanishka, a buddhist emperor who ruled much of north western India in 2nd century AD, also included Gandhara. It was once a flourishing center of Buddhism with many monasteries and universities.

Figure: Location of Taxila in Pakistan. Latitude: 33.7370° N, Longitude: 72.7985° E

Figure: Dharmarajika stupa in Taxila, a Gandhara stupa from 3rd century AD. By Sasha Isachenko – Own work, CC BY-SA 3.0, https://commons.wikimedia.org/w/index.php?curid=23357216x

Figure: Bhir mound in Taxila, site of important excavations related to Taxila university. By Dawoodmajoka – Own work, Public Domain, https://commons.wikimedia.org/w/index.php?curid=5575254

24.1 Taxila

Taxila, about 30 km northwest of Islamabad, was one of the most celebrated cities of the ancient world — the capital of the Gandhara kingdom and a major Buddhist university city.

The famous Chinese pilgrim Fa-Hien (Faxian) visited Taxila in the 5th century CE and described hundreds of monasteries and monks.

The extensive archaeological remains at Taxila include:

- The Dharmarajika Stupa — one of the finest Gandharan stupas, said to enshrine a relic of the Buddha, dating from the time of Ashoka.
- The Jaulian Monastery — a beautifully preserved 5th-century monastic complex.
- The Mohra Moradu Monastery — with remarkable Gandhara stucco figures.
- The Taxila Museum — housing a superb collection of Gandharan Buddhist sculpture, coins, jewellery and other artefacts.

Note: Visitors should check current travel advisories for Pakistan before planning a visit.

*Figure: Kanishka stupa in Shaji ki Dheri in Peshawar. Public Domain,
https://commons.wikimedia.org/w/index.php?curid=151562*

24.2 Shaji ki Dheri in Peshawar

About 7 km from Peshawar city, Shaji ki Dheri is the site of the great
stupa built by the Kushan Emperor Kanishka in the 2nd century CE.
British excavations in 1908–09 uncovered the famous Kanishka
Casket — a relic container inscribed with the king's name — along
with fragments of Buddha statues in the Gandhara style and numerous
coins. The casket is now in the Peshawar Museum.

*Figure: Amlukdara stupa in Swat Valley. By Fazal.Khaliq - Own work,
CC   BY-SA   4.0,   https://commons.wikimedia.org/w/
index.php?curid=51925825*

24.3 Oddiyana in Swat valley

The lush Swat Valley in Khyber Pakhtunkhwa province is identified
by many Vajrayana traditions as Oddiyana — the birthplace of Guru
Padmasambhava, the founder of Tibetan Buddhism. It was an
important centre for Mahayana and Vajrayana Buddhism from the 1st
through the 7th centuries CE, and numerous ruins and rock carvings
survive. The Amlukdara Stupa near Barikot is one of the most

important surviving Buddhist monuments in the valley. Many rock carvings of Buddhas and Bodhisattvas are found along ancient pathways.

24.3 Conclusion

In this chapter, we have discussed the Taxila university, an ancient Buddhist university located in Pakistan and a Kanishka monastery near Peshawar, as well as the Swat valley.

Chapter 25: Planning Your Buddhist Pilgrimage – Suggested Itineraries

In this chapter, we discuss a few practical itineraries to help you plan your journey across the sacred Buddhist sites of the Indian subcontinent. The routes are designed to be spiritually enriching, geographically logical, and mindful of travel constraints.

25.1 Short Pilgrimage Itineraries

These are suitable for travellers for a long weekend or a short break with spiritual depth.

1. Bodhgaya Intensive (Bihar)

Base: Bodhgaya

- Day 1: Arrive in Bodhgaya, visit Mahabodhi Temple, Bodhi Tree, Vajrasana. Evening meditation under the tree.
- Day 2: Visit Sujata Temple & Stupa, Dungeshwari Caves, International temples (Thai, Japanese, Tibetan).
- Day 3: Visit Bodhgaya Museum, Mahabodhi Society Temple, and quiet reflection in Meditation Park.

This is ideal for deep spiritual immersion in the holiest site in Buddhism.

2. Sarnath Mini-Circuit (Uttar Pradesh)

Base: Varanasi

- Day 1: Arrive in Varanasi. Visit Ghats, short Ganga boat ride.
- Day 2: Sarnath: Dhamekh Stupa, Ashoka Pillar,

Archaeological Museum, Mulagandhakuti Vihara.

- Day 3: Visit local monasteries (Tibetan, Japanese, Burmese), and explore Varanasi before departure.

3. Cultural triangle (Sri Lanka)

- Day 1: Drive to Anuradhapura from Colombo (4.5 hours). Explore Anuradhapura with Sri Maha Bodhi Tree, Ruwanwelisaya Stupa, Abhayagiri and Jetavanaramaya monasteries, and Thuparamaya which enshrines Buddha's bone relic. Stay overnight at Anuradhapura
- Day 1 (optional): Sunset at Mihintale—the cradle of Buddhism in Sri Lanka.
- Day 2: Morning drive to Sigiriya Rock Fortress. Climb Sigiriya Rock.
- Day 2: Drive to Dambulla's cave temple (UNESCO world heritage site) which is near Sigiriya. Stay overnight in Sigiriya or Dambulla
- Day 3: Drive to Kandy, explore Kandy's tooth temple Sri Dalada Maligawa, Buddhist museum and other sites. Stay overnight in Kandy
- Day 4: Drive to Polonnaruwa. Explore the ruins and the palace and Gal Vihara.

25.2 Week long or 10-Day Pilgrimage Circuits

This is suitable for those who want to walk the footsteps of the Buddha in India and Nepal.

1. Core Indian Circuit (Uttar Pradesh & Bihar)

This follows the Buddha's life from birth to enlightenment, teaching, and parinirvana.

- Day 1: Arrive in Varanasi
- Day 2–3: Explore Sarnath (Dhamekh Stupa, Museum, Monasteries)
- Day 4–5: Kushinagar (Parinirvana Temple, Ramabhar Stupa, Burmese & Thai Temples)
- Day 6: Travel to Sravasti (Jetavana, Angulimala Stupa)
- Day 7: Full day in Sravasti
- Day 8–10: Bodhgaya (Mahabodhi Temple, Sujata Temple, Dungeshwari Caves, International Temples)

2. Nepal and North India Classic Route

Combines the Buddha's birthplace with his enlightenment and final journey.

- Day 1: Arrive in Kathmandu
- Day 2: Visit Swayambhunath, Boudhanath, Patan temples
- Day 3–4: Travel to Lumbini (Mayadevi Temple, Monastic Zone)
- Day 5: Cross into India – Travel to Kushinagar
- Day 6–7: Explore Kushinagar
- Day 8–10: Bodhgaya highlights

3. South India Vajrayana Trail

Explore lesser-known, serene Vajrayana Buddhist sites.

- Day 1: Arrive in Hyderabad
- Day 2–3: Nagarjunakonda Island & Anupu
- Day 4–5: Amaravati Stupa and Museum
- Day 6: Travel to Odisha
- Day 7–9: Udayagiri, Ratnagiri, Lalitagiri Monasteries
- Day 10: Dhauli Shanti Stupa, return from Bhubaneswar

25.3 Month long Pilgrimage – The Grand Buddhist Circuit

This gives enough time for the full experience— it is ideal for sabbaticals, retreat travelers, or serious pilgrims.

Week 1: Nepal – The Birthplace & the Himalayan Blessings

- Lumbini, Kathmandu valley (Swayambhunath, Boudhanath, Patan), Namo Buddha

Week 2: India – Enlightenment and Teaching

- Bodhgaya (3 days)
- Rajgir (Vulture's Peak, Venu Van)
- Nalanda University
- Sarnath (2 days)

Week 3: India – Buddha's Last Days

- Kushinagar
- Sravasti (Jetavana)
- Vaishali (Stupa & relics)
- Sankissa (Optional)

Week 4: Expansion of the Dharma

- Sanchi Stupa (Madhya Pradesh)
- Ajanta & Ellora Caves (Maharashtra)
- Deekshabhumi in Nagpur (Dr. Ambedkar conversion site)
- Optional: Global Vipassana Pagoda in Mumbai

Add-On Options:

- Bhutan (Paro Tiger's Nest, Thimphu monasteries)

- Sri Lanka (Anuradhapura, Kandy, Dambulla)
- Pakistan (Taxila, Swat Valley)
- Bangladesh (Paharpur)

25.4 Conclusion

In this chapter, we have covewred a few iterenaries which might help travellers or pilgrims plan their travel, depending on the time they have available.

Chapter 26: Conclusion

In this book, we have discussed important Buddhist temples and monasteries located in the countries of the Indian subcontinent: India, Nepal, Sri Lanka, Bangladesh and Pakistan. These sacred lands hold within them the echoes of the Buddha's footsteps, his teachings, and the flourishing of the Dhamma over millennia.

From the Bodhi Tree at Bodhgaya where Siddhartha attained enlightenment, to the serene grounds of Sarnath where he first turned the Wheel of Dhamma, and the quiet forests of Kushinagar where he passed into Mahaparinirvana—we have traced the significant milestones of the Buddha's life. In addition, we have highlighted important sites of later Buddhist expansion such as the cave monasteries at Ajanta, the great stupa at Sanchi, the revivalist energy of Deekshabhumi, and the thriving spiritual communities in places like Bylakuppe and Rumtek.

We also ventured beyond India's borders to sacred locations like Lumbini in Nepal—the Buddha's birthplace, Kandy in Sri Lanka—home of the Tooth Relic, Paro Taktsang in Bhutan—symbolic of Vajrayana mysticism, Paharpur in Bangladesh—testimony to monastic excellence, and Taxila in Pakistan—an ancient seat of learning and spiritual exchange.

The subcontinent is where Buddhism originated and spread to other parts of the world. Hence, many important historical places related to Buddhism are located here. We have not been able to discuss all the places, but only focused on a selection of more important or famous Buddhist places.

It is our hope that this guide inspires not only travel and exploration but also reflection and inner transformation. Each site is more than a destination—it is a doorway to the Dhamma, a chance to pause, contemplate, and rekindle one's connection to the teachings of the Buddha.

Glossary of Buddhist Terms

The following is a brief guide to key Buddhist terms used in this book.

Abhidhamma / Abhidharma — The third 'basket' (pitaka) of the Pali/Sanskrit Buddhist canon, dealing with systematic philosophical and psychological analysis.

Arahant (Pali) / Arhat (Sanskrit) — A person who has attained full liberation from suffering and the cycle of rebirth; the ideal of early Buddhism.

Bodhi — Awakening or enlightenment; the full understanding of the nature of reality that constitutes liberation in Buddhism.

Bodhisattva — In Mahayana Buddhism, a being who has vowed to attain Buddhahood for the benefit of all sentient beings.

Chaitya / Chaitya Griha — A prayer hall or shrine containing a stupa; a rock-cut Buddhist temple.

Dagoba — Sri Lankan term for a stupa.

Dhamma / Dharma — The teachings of the Buddha; also, the natural law or truth that the Buddha discovered and taught.

Dhyani Buddhas — The five Meditation Buddhas of Vajrayana Buddhism, each associated with a direction and a specific quality of enlightened mind.

Dzong — A type of fortress-monastery found in Bhutan and parts of Tibet.

Gelugpa — One of the four main schools of Tibetan Buddhism; the school of the Dalai Lamas.

Jataka — Stories of the previous lives of the Buddha, illustrating the development of the ten perfections (paramitas).

Kora — Circumambulation of a sacred site, done in a clockwise direction.

Mahaparinirvana — The final, complete nirvana of the Buddha at his death.

Mahayana — The 'Great Vehicle' tradition of Buddhism; dominant in Tibet, China, Japan and Korea.

Mudra — A symbolic hand gesture used in Buddhist iconography and ritual.

Nibbana / **Nirvana** — The extinguishing of craving, aversion and delusion; the goal of Buddhist practice.

Nyingma — The oldest of the four main schools of Tibetan Buddhism.

Pali — The ancient Indian language in which the Theravada scriptures (Tipitaka) are preserved.

Sakya — One of the four main schools of Tibetan Buddhism.

Sangha — The community of Buddhist monks, nuns and lay practitioners.

Stupa / **Dagoba** / **Pagoda** — A domed or tiered monument enshrining relics or commemorating sacred events; the characteristic architectural form of Buddhism.

Sutra / **Sutta** — A discourse of the Buddha (Sanskrit: sutra; Pali: sutta).

Tathagata — A title of the Buddha meaning 'one who has thus gone'; used by the Buddha to refer to himself.

Thangka — A Tibetan Buddhist painting on cloth, depicting deities, mandalas or scenes from sacred narratives.

Theravada — The 'Way of the Elders'; the oldest surviving school of Buddhism; dominant in Sri Lanka, Myanmar, Thailand, Laos and Cambodia.

Tipitaka / Tripitaka — The 'Three Baskets': the complete canon of Buddhist scriptures, comprising the Vinaya, the Suttas/Sutras and the Abhidhamma/Abhidharma.

Torana — An ornamental gateway, particularly the carved gateways of the Sanchi stupa.

Vajrasana — The 'Diamond Throne'; the stone seat at Bodhgaya marking the exact spot of the Buddha's enlightenment.

Vajrayana — The 'Diamond Vehicle'; the tantric tradition of Buddhism prevalent in Tibet, Bhutan, Nepal and parts of Japan.

Vihara — A Buddhist monastery.

Vipassana — Insight meditation; direct observation of the three characteristics of existence through sustained mindfulness.

About the authors

Joy Bose is a data scientist by profession. He has travelled to many Buddhist sites and other culturally important sites in Asia over several years, and has a keen interest in Buddhist meditation. He lives in Bangalore.

Siva Prasad Bose is an author of introductory guidebooks on aspects of Indian laws. He is currently retired after many years of service as an electrical engineer in Uttar Pradesh Power Corporation Limited. He received his engineering degree from Jadavpur University, Kolkata and has a law degree from Meerut University, Meerut and a BSc from MMH College, Ghaziabad. His interests lie in the fields of family law, civil law, law of contracts, and areas of law related to power electricity related issues. He lives in Delhi.

Other Books by Siva Prasad Bose

Introduction to Wills and Probate

Senior Citizens Abuse in India

Introduction to Negotiable Instruments

Introduction to Marriage Laws in India

Neighbor Problems in India and what to do about them

Delays in Court Cases in India

Self-Publish Books and E-Books in India

Introduction to Patents and Patent Law in India

Introduction to Property Law in India

Did you love *Guide to Buddhist Sites in the Indian Subcontinent*? Then you should read *Wearable Gadgets and Technology for Meditation*[1] by Joy Bose and Siva Prasad Bose!

[2]

Meditation is as old as mankind. It needs almost no props, save a cushion, some instructions and an intent to meditate. It gives a number of benefits ranging from increased happiness, stress relief, a better immune system, better concentration, enhanced quality of life and so on. Some might even say it gives insight into the nature of things as they really are.

We live in the technology age, where life is more fast paced than ever before and there exist a range of distractions. Many would say technology has made us more disconnected from nature and from the real world. However, technology can also be used as a tool for aiding

---

1. https://books2read.com/u/4jNXJD

2. https://books2read.com/u/4jNXJD

meditation or enhancing the meditation and well-being experience, partly thanks to the variety of technologies such as EEG, tDCS, PEMF, binaural beats that can be leveraged in wearable devices.

In this book, we explore a variety of wearable gadgets and apps that can help in meditation and enhancing well-being and happiness. We also share the authors' experience in using some of these apps and gadgets.

It is hoped that learning about these will encourage the readers to try out some of them, and utilize them to improve their own meditation.

About the Author

Joy Bose is a data scientist and software engineer by profession. He lives and works in Bangalore, India. He has practiced meditation in multiple traditions including mindfulness meditation and Vajrayana, and is keenly interested in applications of technology in the field of meditation.